PRESSURE COOKER COOKBOOK

Easy Stews Recipes for Your Electric Pressure Cooker

(Affordable & Easy-to-prepare Recipes for Fast and Flavorful Meals)

Emma Holt

Published by Sharon Lohan

© **Emma Holt**

All Rights Reserved

Pressure Cooker Cookbook: Easy Stews Recipes for Your Electric Pressure Cooker (Affordable & Easy-to-prepare Recipes for Fast and Flavorful Meals)

ISBN 978-1-990334-22-1

All rights reserved. No part of this guide may be reproduced in any form without permission in writing from the publisher except in the case of brief quotations embodied in critical articles or reviews.

Legal & Disclaimer

The information contained in this book is not designed to replace or take the place of any form of medicine or professional medical advice. The information in this book has been provided for educational and entertainment purposes only.

The information contained in this book has been compiled from sources deemed reliable, and it is accurate to the best of the Author's knowledge; however, the Author cannot guarantee its accuracy and validity and cannot be held liable for any errors or omissions. Changes are periodically made to this book. You must consult your doctor or get professional medical advice before using any of the suggested remedies, techniques, or information in this book.

Table of contents

Part 1 1

Introduction 2

Chapter 1- Mixture of Pressure 6

1. Pork Roast 6
2. Pressure Cooker Whole Chicken 8
3. Pressure Cooked Artichokes 9
4. Pressure Cooked Hard Boiled Eggs 10
5. Ham & Navy Bean Soup 11

Chapter 2- Mixture of Pressure 12

6. Caribbean Oxtail & Beans 12
7. Pressure Cooker Barbeque Chicken 14
8. Pressure Cooker Potato Salad 16
9. Pressure Cooker Quinoa 18
10. Spicy Ribs 19

Chapter 3- Mixture of Pressure 21

11. Chow Mein 21
12. Spring Meatballs 23
13. Spicy Italian Chicken & Sausage 25
14. Ribs, Beer & Honey 27
15. Cooked Beef with Dumplings 29

Chapter 4- Pressure Cooker Fish 31
16. Pressure Cooker Fish Fillets 31
17. Sweet & Sour Shrimps 33
18. Fish Steak & Mushrooms 35
19. Fish Broth 37
20. Salmon Steaks 39
Chapter 5- Pressure Cooker Poultry 40
21. Turkey & Lentil 40
22. Braised Duck 42
23. Chicken in Lemon Sauce 43
24. French Style Chicken in Wine Sauce 45
25. Ginger Chicken 48
Chapter 6- Pressure Cooker Vegetable 50
26. Stuffed Tomatoes 50
27. Stuffed Green Peppers 52
28. Spicy Paneer 54
29. Curry 56
30. Egg, Corn Soup 58
Date & Apple Pudding 60
Lemon Creme 62
Carrot Halva 64
Chocolate Souffle 65

Apple Walnut Bread Desert	67
Conclusion	69
Part 2	70
Introduction	71
Pressure Cooking	72
Pressure cooking tips and tricks	74
Chicken	77
Chicken in Honeyed Vinaigrette	77
BBQ Chicken	78
Spicy Lime Chicken Strips	80
Sour Cream Chicken	81
Herbed Chicken	83
Beef	84
Hearty Beef Ribs	84
Citrus and Ginger Beef	85
Classic Beef and Mushroom	86
Pot Roast and Buttered Potatoes	87
Pineapple Beef Teriyaki	89
Pork	90
Home-cooked Sweet Ham	90
Soy and Ginger Pork Chops	91
Adobo Pork Stew	92

Pork Roast 93

Cranberry Pork Cutlets 94

Seafood 95

Seafood Stew 95

Snapper in Sesame Soy Sauce 97

Coconut Halibut Stew 98

Celery and Shrimp Stew 99

Shrimp Marinara with Spaghetti 100

Snacks and Starters 101

Garlic and Herb Creamy Potatoes 101

Babaganoush and Crackers 103

Buttered Baby Carrots 105

Baby Rosemary Potatoes 106

Tomato and Green Beans 107

Baked Beans 108

Spicy Chicken Spread 109

Hearty Bowl of Chili 110

Sour Cream Potatoes and Chives 111

Chips n' Dip 112

PORK and BEEF 113

Pork Chops 113

Creamy Pork Chops 115

Spanish Braised Pork	117
Pork Chop Suey	118
Beer Braised Ribs	120
Beef Roll-Ups	121
Apple Cider Pork Chops	123
Split Pea and Ham Soup	125
Mushroom Beef Stew	126
Pressure Cooked Meatballs	128
CHICKEN	130
Whole Chicken	130
Chicken Vegetable Soup	131
Chicken and Rice Soup	133
Cranberry Chicken	134
Hungarian Chicken	135
Chicken Piccata	136
Chicken Cacciatore	138
Chicken Curry	141
Raspberry Chicken	143
Kentucky Fried Chicken	145
VEGETABLES	147
Butternut Squash Soup	149
White Bean Dip	151

Garlic Mashed Potatoes 153
Tomato Soup 155
Tortellini Minestrone Soup 157
Chickpea Curry 159
Lemon Ginger Honey 161
Pressure Cooked Salsa 162
Clam Chowder from New England 163
French Soupy Onion 165
Awesome Irish Stew 167
Super Duper Spaghetti Sauce 169
Italian Mystery Soup 172
VEGETABLES & SIDE DISH 174
Butternut Risotto Beauty 174
Quinoa Queens Pilaf 177
Pure Rice Pilaf 179
Cocktail Curvy Onions 181
MAIN COURSE 183
Cooker Magic with Chicken Sauce 183
Cooker Perfect Carnitas 186

Part 1

Introduction

You are really going to enjoy trying out this great collection of pressure cooker recipes. Included in this book is a bonus collection of desert recipes that I am sure you and your loved ones will enjoy! It is always a good idea to find new ways to keep your mind stimulated, and this certainly includes learning new ways to prepare your foods.

Using a pressure cooker to prepare your foods is an amazing method that everyone should try. It is unlike any other way that you have prepared your meals in the past. Using a pressure cooker is a form of cooking that is in a class of its own. It may seem a bit strange to you at first as you will have to get used to the fact that it is sealed so that you cannot take the lid on and off throughout the cooking of the food.

Also keep in mind the top six benefits to pressure cooking your food:

1. Your food will retain most of its nutrients making them tastier.
2. Saves time when it comes to preparing meals, cook time is greatly reduced.
3. It is a great energy saver, it is much more efficient that having multiple pots on separate burners. Pressure

cookers tend to offer more of one-pot cooking recipes in general.

4. It keeps your kitchen cooler, a pressure cooker retains the heat and steam resulting in a cooler kitchen.

5. Less cleaning is involved with a pressure cooker, you won't have the spray that you get from other pots and pans messing up the surrounding areas. The pressure cooker is a secured pot that prevents spatters and splashes from occurring.

6. You can also use your pressure cooker to preserve food so that you can use them at a later date by canning foods. You can get larger models to use for holding more jars the larger models are referred to as "canners."

I am sure like most people you are used to taking the lid of your pot and tasting your special meal you are preparing during the cooking process. You will be learning a whole new approach that this step is not included. Learning the art of proper pressure cooking requires a certain amount of knowledge that the average person does not have. But you are all set to pressure cook your way into some tasty meals to serve to your loved ones, you are now armed with this easy to follow pressure cooker cookbook.

Following the instructions in this cookbook you will be able to make some great dishes that will have your loved wants asking for seconds. You will find that preparing meals with your pressure cooker will give you time to do other things besides standing over a hot stove for two or three hours. You will be able to leave the pressure cooker and let it take care of cooking the meal while you are able to perhaps spend time with you loved ones.

The recipes that are in this book are not only great tasting, but they are also quick and easy to prepare. You will be able to take inexpensive cuts of meat and by cooking them in your pressure cooker you will make them taste so yummy and tender. You will have the freedom to get other things done while the pressure cooker cooks the meal or just sit down and relax for a while.

Use the recipes in this cookbook as a base, don't be afraid to add things that you enjoy into the recipe. Make it your own by adding your own special ingredients to the recipe. This is how you can build some wonderful recipes that you and your loved ones can enjoy over a lifetime. When your children are grown they can take their favorite pressure cooker recipes with them. Perhaps as a house warming gift you can get them their own pressure cooker when they leave home. But for now we will stick to the present and make some great pressure cooker meals for you and your loved ones using this cookbook to guide you through a new level in the cooking experience that you are sure to love! Now it is time to open these pages and choose the first recipe that you will make using your pressure cooker—the beginning of many tasty meals to come!

Chapter 1- Mixture of Pressure

1. Pork Roast

Total Time Needed: one hour

Ingredients:

- three pounds of pork loin, boneless
- half a teaspoon of dry mustard
- half a teaspoon of sage
- half a teaspoon of sea salt
- two teaspoons of paprika
- two cups of Leeks, chopped
- one teaspoon of coconut oil
- one teaspoon of parsley, dried
- one teaspoon of garlic, minced
- two cups of chicken broth
- two cups of water
- one teaspoon of ground black pepper
- one red onion, minced
- half a teaspoon of thyme

Directions:

Add oil to the bottom of cooker and allow to heat on high. Add pork roast to the heated oil and allow to brown on all sides. Set aside and allow to cool. Add garlic, leeks, onions and cook for five minutes until soft. Pour your water and broth in and allow to heat. In a bowl mix spices together, mustard, thyme, pepper, sage, paprika, parsley. Rub roast with spice mix, then place into liquid in your cooker. Secure the lid and allow the cooker to rise to high pressure. Once it is at high pressure cook for 45 minutes. Release the lid to cool the pressure cooker, and serve.

2. Pressure Cooker Whole Chicken

Total Time Needed: 30 minutes

Ingredients:

- two pound whole chicken
- pepper and salt to taste
- two tablespoons of coconut oil
- one and a half cups of chicken broth
- one teaspoon of poultry seasoning

Directions:

Rinse the chicken then use hand towels to pat it dry. Mix seasoning—pepper, salt, and poultry seasoning in bowl, then add to chicken. Set your oil to heat in the pressure cooker when it is hot brown the season on all sides then set aside. Put a food rack inside your pressure cooker, place chicken on top. Pour broth around the chicken the secure lid of pressure cooker. Once the pressure cooker has raised to high pressure allow to cook for 25 minutes. Remove the cooker from the flame and allow it to cool under running water to release the lid. Carve up the chicken and enjoy with a favorite side dish.

3. Pressure Cooked Artichokes

Total Time Needed: 20 minutes

Ingredients:

- eight baby artichokes
- two tablespoons of coconut oil
- one lemon
- four cloves of garlic, diced

Directions:

Trim the tops of your artichokes. Dice the garlic cloves and put the pieces in between the artichoke leaves. Then place them into a steamer basket in your pressure cooker. Add a slice of lemon with the artichokes in the cooker. Drizzle with melted coconut oil. Secure the lid and allow it to rise to high pressure. Once it is at high pressure cook for 12 minutes. Cool the cooker by running under cool water. Garnish artichokes with lemon slices and serve.

4. Pressure Cooked Hard Boiled Eggs

Total Time Needed: 15 minutes

Ingredients:

- two cups of water
- eight eggs

Directions:

Pour the water into your pressure cooker, place steamer tray into cooker and place your eggs on the steamer tray, make sure basket is above water. Secure the lid and allow to rise to low pressure. Once at that point allow eggs to cook for six minutes. Remove pressure cooker from heat and let stand for five minutes. Cool pressure cooker under cold running water, carefully open the lid. Peel the eggs and serve.

5. Ham & Navy Bean Soup

Total Time Needed: 40 minutes

Ingredients:

- one quarter cup of minced green pepper
- four pieces of celery, sliced
- four carrots, sliced
- two teaspoons of sea salt
- half a cup of coconut oil, melted
- four cups of dried navy beans, pre-soaked
- three pounds of ham shanks
- two cups of tomato sauce
- one teaspoon of garlic, minced
- pepper to taste
- three quarts of water

Directions:

Discard the liquid that you were soaking the beans in. Pour all of your ingredients into the pressure cooker and secure the lid. Cook for 30 minutes on high pressure. Allow the pressure cooker to cool down on its own. Serve and enjoy this yummy soup!

Chapter 2- Mixture of Pressure

6. Caribbean Oxtail & Beans

Total Time Needed: 1 1/4 hours

Ingredients:

- one large onion, chopped
- one pound of oxtail, chopped
- one green onion, thinly sliced
- one teaspoon of ginger root, fresh
- one sprig of thyme, chopped
- two tablespoons of soy sauce
- one Scotch Bonnet pepper, chopped
- half a teaspoon of sea salt
- one teaspoon of ground black pepper
- two tablespoons of coconut oil, melted
- one and a half cups of water and another separate two tablespoons of water
- one cup of Fava beans, drained
- one teaspoon of allspice berries
- one tablespoon of cornstarch

Directions:

In a large mixing bowl combine your green onion garlic, thyme, ginger, soy sauce, pepper, and oxtail. Toss and massage oxtail. In a large skillet heat the oil and brown the oxtail pieces on all sides over a medium high heat. Put into the pressure cooker once browned. Add water. Secure the lid and allow it to rise to high pressure. Once at high pressure allow it to cook for 25 minutes. Remove the cooker from heat and allow to cool naturally then remove the lid carefully. Put in the beans and allspice. Create a slurry with two tablespoons of water and cornstarch. Mix this into the pressure cooker and stir well.

7. Pressure Cooker Barbeque Chicken

Total Time Needed: 45 minutes

Ingredients:

- three chicken breast halves with bone
- two teaspoons of chicken bouillon
- one twelve ounce can of beer
- half a cup of water
- one teaspoon of Nutmeg
- one teaspoon of Cinnamon
- half a teaspoon of Ginger
- two teaspoons of salt
- one eighth teaspoon of fresh ground pepper
- barbeque sauce of your choosing

Directions:

Add ginger, nutmeg, cinnamon, salt, and pepper into a container. Put the chicken into the container and massage. Proceed to pour your water, beer, and chicken bouillon into the pressure cooker. Add your seasoned chicken to the liquid in the pressure cooker and allow to rise to high pressure over a high flame. Cook at high pressure for 20 minutes. Allow the cooker to cool down naturally then grill for 10 minutes. Brush on barbeque sauce and grill for another five minutes and enjoy!

8. Pressure Cooker Potato Salad

Total Time Needed: One and a half hours

Ingredients:

- one stalk of celery, chopped
- one quarter cup of red onion, chopped
- one cup of water
- six red potatoes, scrubbed, and chopped
- one teaspoon of apple cider vinegar
- one teaspoon of Dijon Mustard
- half a cup of Mayonnaise
- one tablespoon of dill, fresh, chopped
- three hard-boiled eggs, chopped
- salt and pepper to taste
- half a cup of sweet pickles, finely diced

Directions:

Pour water and potatoes into your pressure cooker. Securely close the lid and allow to rise to high pressure over a high flame. Cook for about five minutes. Remove the cooker from the flame and cool under cold running water. Peel and dice potatoes, layer them with celery, and onion. Season with salt and pepper, add dill, and chopped eggs. In a separate bowl combine vinegar, pickles, mustard, and mayonnaise. Fold this mixture gently into the potatoes. Chill for at least one hour.

9. Pressure Cooker Quinoa

Total Time Needed: 15 minutes

Ingredients:

- two cups of whole grain quinoa
- two tablespoons of coconut oil, melted
- one teaspoon of garlic, minced
- two teaspoons of Turmeric
- three cups of water
- one teaspoon of sea salt
- two teaspoons of Cumin
- Herbs, fresh to garnish

Directions:

Empty quinoa into a fine mesh strainer and rinse under running water, rub the grains in the strainer. Preheat your pressure cooker over medium heat, pour in oil, add garlic, and saute until soft. Mix in your cumin, turmeric, and salt. Pour in your water then add the quinoa. Securely close lid, allow to rise to high pressure, heat over low flame for a minute. Allow to cool naturally and then open and tumble and fluff quinoa and serve.

10. Spicy Ribs

Total Time Needed: 30 minutes

Ingredients:

- one tablespoon of brown sugar
- four tablespoons of red wine
- two tablespoons of Worcestershire sauce
- three cups of ketchup
- one tablespoon of almond flour
- one cup of water
- one large onion, chopped
- one teaspoon of Dijon Mustard
- two teaspoons of chili powder
- one teaspoon of sea salt
- one teaspoon of black ground pepper
- two tablespoons of coconut oil
- one teaspoon of garlic, minced

Directions:

In a bowl mix ingredients except for ribs, oil, onion, water, and flour. Add ribs to mix and stir thoroughly, and marinate in fridge for four hours. Divide the ribs into two portions and save the marinade for later. Heat the oil in the fast cooker for about two minutes; fry the beef in batches from all sides. With the remaining oil after frying, add onions, and then fry until they brown. Add ribs, marinade, one cup of water, and mix. Close the pressure cooker, bring to a full power using high heat. Reduce the heat and cook for 30 minutes. Remove them from heat and put them aside to cool. Open the pressure cooker, arrange ribs on plates, and remove grease from cooker. In a separate bowl, gradually add the one cup of water to flour, while stirring the flour constantly with remaining fluid in pressure cooker, whisk constantly. Put the pressure cooker on medium heat and cook the sauce for three minutes, keep stirring as it cooks. Pour the sauce over the ribs and serve warm.

Chapter 3- Mixture of Pressure

11. Chow Mein

Total Time Needed: 25 minutes

Ingredients:

- one teaspoon of garlic, minced
- two teaspoons of almond flour
- two eggs
- two ounces of mushrooms, sliced
- seven ounces of cabbage, sliced
- two stalks of celery, cut into slices
- seven ounces of chicken breast, boned, and skinned
- salt to taste
- seven tablespoons of peanut oil
- two teaspoons of apple cider vinegar
- two teaspoons of tomato sauce
- two teaspoons of chili sauce
- two teaspoons of soy sauce
- one inch of ginger piece, cut into slices
- seven ounces of noodles
- one leek, trimmed, and sliced
- half a cup of chicken broth

Directions:

Rinse chicken then cook in the pressure cooker with half a cup of water for ten minutes. Save the broth and cut the chicken into strips. Pour three cups of water into pot, add noodles, and salt. Close the pressure cooker and bring it to full power on high heat. Reduce the heat to medium and cook for five minutes. Remove from heat then open pressure cooker to remove built up steam. Pour cold water over pasta in strainer, leave to cool. In a skillet, heat one tablespoon of oil, pour lightly beaten eggs, and stir-fry until dense. Cut the omelet into strips and remove from pan. Now heat two tablespoons of oil in same pan and saute garlic, leeks, cabbage, mushrooms, ginger, and chicken. Add half a cup of chicken broth mixed with soy sauce and almond flour. Simmer until it thickens. Add tomato sauce, chili sauce, and vinegar. In a different pan, heat cooked noodles with remaining oil. Transfer to a platter and garnish with strips of omelet; pour over the sauce, chicken, and vegetables, serve hot.

12. Spring Meatballs

Total Time Needed: 12 minutes

Ingredients:

- one pound of lean ground beef
- half a pound of ground pork
- one teaspoon of grated lemon peel
- one teaspoon of paprika
- one teaspoon of salt
- one small onion, finely chopped
- two eggs
- two slices of whole wheat bread soaked in water, and squeezed
- two tablespoons of chive
- six tablespoons of almond flour
- six tablespoons of butter
- three cups of natural vegetable broth
- five tablespoons of parsley, chopped
- four teaspoons of freshly squeezed lemon juice

Directions:

In a bowl mix all the ingredients except for half of the lemon juice, butter, broth, chives, and flour. Divide the mixture to 24 portions and form balls of about 4 centimetres in diameter. Pour the broth into the pressure cooker, bring it to a boil over high heat, and add the meatballs one by one. Close the pressure cooker and bring to full power over high heat. Reduce heat and cook for four minutes. Remove the pressure cooker from the heat and allow to cool slowly. Open the pressure cooker, place meatballs on plates, and keep warm. Strain the remaining liquid after cooking and save it for later. Melt the butter in the pressure cooker over medium heat. Add flour and cook over low heat, stirring constantly for about four minutes. Remove from heat and gradually add the preserved liquid to it. Put the pressure cooker on medium heat. Boil and stir constantly until the sauce thickens. Add the remaining lemon juice, and parsley. Serve with warm pasta or rice.

13. Spicy Italian Chicken & Sausage

Total Time Needed: 40

Ingredients:

- two red peppers, sliced
- one onion, diced
- two chicken breasts, sliced, skinless, and boneless
- four Italian sausages
- one tablespoon of coconut oil
- one teaspoon of garlic, minced
- two tablespoons of red wine vinegar
- 16 ounces of tomatoes, diced
- salt and pepper to taste
- red pepper flakes
- one quarter teaspoon of Fennel seeds
- three quarter teaspoon of Basil

Directions:

Heat your oil in your pressure cooker. While oil is heating skin your sausages. Add chicken and sausages to hot oil brown on all sides. Dice onion, slice peppers. Remove browned meat from the cooker. Add vegetables to heated cooker, allow them to cook until they have become soft. Add vinegar and stir. Add chicken, sausage, tomatoes, fennel, basil, red pepper, salt and pepper. Secure the lid on the pressure cooker allow to rise to high pressure. Once at high pressure reduce the heat so pressure will stabilize and cook for another ten minutes. Allow the cooker to cool, open lid, and serve.

14. Ribs, Beer & Honey

Total Time Needed: 25 minutes

Ingredients:

- two pounds of ribs
- two tablespoons of coconut oil
- one cup of organic honey
- one cup of non-alcoholic beer
- one teaspoon of Dijon mustard
- one teaspoon of chili powder
- one teaspoon of lemon juice, fresh squeezed
- one teaspoon of sage
- two teaspoons of sea salt

Directions:

Divide the ribs into three parts. Heat your oil in the pressure cooker for two minutes, fry ribs in batches on all sides. Remove the pressure cooker from heat and remove grease. Add the ribs and the rest of the ingredients while stirring. Close the pressure cooker and bring to its full power over high heat. Reduce to medium heat and cook for twenty minutes. Remove the pressure cooker from heat and leave to cool slowly. Open the pressure cooker arrange the ribs on serving dishes, and keep them warm. Remove grease from liquid that remained after cooking. Put pressure cooker on medium heat and cook until the sauce's volume is reduced by half then pour over ribs and serve.

15. Cooked Beef with Dumplings

Total Time Needed: 20 minutes

Ingredients:

- one pound of beef loin, cut into cubes, two inches in size
- salt and pepper to taste
- one bay leaf
- two large onions, sliced
- two large carrots, sliced into strips
- half a cup of beef broth

Dumplings:

- a pinch of baking powder
- four ounces of almond flour
- one medium onion chopped
- one tablespoon of parsley, chopped
- salt and pepper to taste

Directions:

Dumplings: Mix all of the ingredients, add some water, and knead as dough. Form twelve small balls. Boil six fluid ounces of water in pressure cooker and add the dumplings. Close the pressure cooker and bring to its full power over high heat. Reduce the heat to a minimum and cook for eight minutes. Open immediately after the release of the steam. Remove dumplings from the pot.

Beef: Pour half a cup of beef broth in the pressure cooker. Add beef, onion, bay leaf, salt and pepper. Close the pressure cooker and bring to its full power over high heat. Reduce heat to a medium heat and cook for 15 minutes. Leave the pressure cooker to cool slowly. Once cooled open and add carrots. Close the pressure cooker and bring to its full power over high heat. Reduce heat to minimum and cook for three minutes. Once again leave the pressure cooker to cool slowly before opening. Serve warm with dumplings.

Chapter 4- Pressure Cooker Fish

16. Pressure Cooker Fish Fillets

Total Time Needed: 10 minutes

Ingredients:

- three cups of mushrooms, thinly sliced
- 6 sole fillets
- two tablespoons of lemon juice
- salt and pepper to taste
- three tablespoons of organic butter
- half of small red onion, finely chopped
- two cloves garlic, finely chopped
- one cup of celery, finely chopped
- three cups of water
- one teaspoon of thyme, ground
- one handful of dill, fresh
- four green olives, pitted, and sliced
- one large tomato, peeled, and sliced
- one cup of dry white wine

Directions:

Rub the fish with lemon juice, pepper, and salt, marinate for one hour. Melt butter in a saucepan, add garlic, onion, and celery. Stir-fry until onion is slightly browned. Add mushrooms and wine; cook until the wine evaporates. Add tomato, olives, dill and some salt. Cook until the fluid has evaporated. Place each fillet on a piece of aluminium foil. Evenly spread the mixture over fish and wrap foil around the fish. Fold the top and sides to form packets. Pour water into the pressure cooker and put rack or inset into cooker. Place the fish packets on top of inset. Close the pressure cooker and bring to full pressure on high heat. Reduce the heat and cook for three minutes. Remove the pressure cooker from heat and release the steam. Open the pressure cooker and arrange the fish on to serving plates and enjoy!

17. Sweet & Sour Shrimps

Total Time Needed: 10 minutes

Ingredients:

- one stalk of celery, cut into diagonal strips
- eight ounces of shrimp, deveined, and cleaned
- four ounces of cucumber, cut into diagonal strips
- three yellow peppers, cut into strips
- two medium carrots, cut into diagonal strips
- one leek, cut into diagonal strips
- two cups of peanut oil
- salt to taste

Sauce:

- one teaspoon of sugar
- two tablespoons of cornstarch
- two tablespoons of tomato sauce
- four teaspoons of soy sauce
- four teaspoons of organic honey
- one cup of apple cider vinegar

Dough:

- two tablespoons of almond flour
- one teaspoon of baking powder

- two eggs
- one cup of milk

Directions:

In the pressure cooker and a cup of water and add the cleaned shrimp. Close the pressure cooker and bring to full boil on high heat. Reduce the heat to medium and cook for five minutes. Remove the pressure cooker from heat and open to allow steam to be released. Remove the shrimps and drain. Prepare the dough, beat eggs, add flour, and milk. Finally add salt, and baking powder. Add it bit of water to get it like batter-like dough. In a pan heat oil, dip shrimps in batter and fry until golden and crispy. Remove the shrimp and stir-fry the vegetables, drying them on paper towel. In a skillet mix flour, salt, sugar, vinegar, honey, soy sauce, and tomato sauce. Add the vegetables and shrimp; bring to boil and heat for four minutes, then enjoy.

18. Fish Steak & Mushrooms

Total Time Needed: 10 minutes

Ingredients:

- one inch piece of ginger, freshly grated
- one tablespoon of sugar
- one teaspoon of sea salt
- two large pieces of halibut steaks, two centimetres thick
- one cup of mushrooms, thinly sliced
- one cup of shallots, with chives, chopped
- save one tablespoon of chives for garnish
- three tablespoons of soy sauce
- one cup of dry white wine
- one tablespoon of white wine vinegar

Directions:

In a shallow bowl, mix all ingredients except fish, mushrooms, and shallots. Add fish steaks, dip them in the sauce, and marinate for one hour. Place the insert into the cooker and place fish on top of it. Pour the marinade into the cooker, place the mushrooms, and onions on top of fish. Close the pressure cooker and bring to full pressure on high heat. Reduce heat and cook for five minutes. Remove from heat and release steam. Open the pressure cooker and arrange fish and vegetables on a serving platter. Remove the inset from pressure cooker. Place the pressure cooker over high heat and cook until the liquid is reduced to half. Stir occasionally then pour over fish and serve warm. Garnish with shallots and chives.

19. Fish Broth

Total Time Needed: 15 minutes

Ingredients:

- half a cup of celery, chopped
- one small carrot, chopped
- one small onion, chopped
- two tablespoons of organic butter
- one bay leaf
- one sprig of parsley
- pinch of white pepper
- one teaspoon of sea salt
- one teaspoon of thyme, dried
- 24 ounces of fish fillets, white non-greasy fish, with bones removed
- six pieces of asparagus, trimmed, and halved.

Directions:

Melt the butter in pressure cooker. Add onion, carrots, celery, and asparagus. Stir-fry until onion gets glossy. Add remaining ingredients and mix. Close the pressure cooker and bring to its full pressure over high heat. Reduce heat and cook for 15 minutes. Remove the pressure cooker from heat and leave to slowly cool.

Open the pressure cooker and strain the broth through a fine sieve.

20. Salmon Steaks

Total Time Needed: 10 minutes

Ingredients:

- two twenty-eight ounce salmon steaks, about one inch thick
- one medium onion, sliced into rings
- one lemon, sliced
- one eighth teaspoon of pepper
- one teaspoon of sea salt
- one cup of dry white wine
- tablespoon of dill, fresh, chopped

Directions:

Put the inset into the pressure cooker and arrange the onion on it. Place the fish on the onion and drizzle with white wine. Season with salt and pepper, arrange lemon slices on the fish, save four slices to garnish serving plates. Close the pressure cooker and bring to full pressure on high heat. Reduce the heat and cook for six minutes. Remove the pressure cooker from heat and release the steam. Open the pressure cooker arrange fish on serving plates and remove the onion, and lemon. Serve warm with lemon slices on top and sprinkled with fresh dill.

Chapter 5- Pressure Cooker Poultry

21. Turkey & Lentil

Total Time Needed: 5 minutes

Ingredients:

- one cup of brown rice
- half a cup of red lentils, Egyptian don't need to be soaked
- half a red pepper, sliced
- half a green pepper, sliced
- 18 ounce turkey thigh, rinsed, drained, cut into strips
- one onion, chopped
- half of a leek, cut into long strips
- one stalk of celery, chopped
- half a cup of mushrooms, thinly sliced
- a couple of leaves of savoy cabbage
- two and a half cups of chicken broth
- one bay leaf
- sea salt, pepper, and paprika to taste
- Bechamel-cheese sauce
- four tablespoons of olive oil
- one tablespoon or so of almond flour

Directions:

Season the turkey strip and gently sprinkle with flour and saute in oil that is preheated in pressure cooker. Add onions, and continue to fry. Add rice and lentils as well as other remaining ingredients. Then pour in chicken broth. Close the pressure cooker and bring to boil. Reduce heat and cook for another three minutes. Then serve and enjoy!

22. Braised Duck

Total Time Needed: 15 minutes

Ingredients:

- thirty five ounce duck, with bones, removed, and sliced
- one lemon
- one ounce of organic butter
- five ounces of vegetable bouillon
- one tablespoon of rosemary
- ten fluid ounces of Worcestershire sauce

Directions:

In the pressure cooker melt your butter and saute the duck until browned on all sides. Add Worcestershire sauce, seasonings, and broth. Close the pressure cooker and bring to full power boiling over high heat. Reduce heat to medium and cook for 15 minutes. Leave the pressure cooker to cool slowly. Open and serve with slices of fresh lemon.

23. Chicken in Lemon Sauce

Total Time Needed: 15 minutes

Ingredients:

- three pounds of skinless chicken
- one large onion, chopped
- two tablespoons of butter
- four cups of chicken broth
- one teaspoon of thyme, dried
- one teaspoon of pepper
- two teaspoons of sea salt
- one cup of celery, chopped
- three tablespoons of lemon juice
- one tablespoon of grated lemon peel
- four tablespoons of almond flour
- one tablespoon of parsley, freshly chopped
- one lemon, sliced

Directions:

Rub chicken with two tablespoons of lemon juice then set aside for one hour. Put the chicken and remaining lemon juice into pressure cooker. Add other ingredients except for butter, flour and parsley. Mix well. Close the pressure cooker and bring to full power over high heat. Reduce the heat to medium and cook for eight minutes. Remove the pressure cooker from heat and leave to cool slowly. Open the pressure cooker; put chicken on a plate, keep warm. Strain the liquid, strain the fat and keep the liquid. Melt butter in pressure cooker on medium heat. Add flour and cook over low heat while whisking. Remove from heat and keep stirring, gradually add preserved liquid throw in lemon slices and mix. Put pressure cooker on medium heat. Cook for about four minutes until the sauce thickens. Pour sauce over chicken garnish with parsley and serve.

24. French Style Chicken in Wine Sauce

Total Time Needed: 15 minutes

Ingredients:

- one cup plus three tablespoons of almond flour
- five tablespoons of butter
- two pounds of chicken, sliced
- three ounces of ham, cut into parts or two inch cubes
- two cloves
- six shallots, peeled
- black pepper to taste
- one teaspoon of sea salt
- two tablespoons of water
- one teaspoon of garlic, minced
- one cup of chicken broth
- one cup of Burgundy wine
- three cups of mushrooms, finely chopped
- one bay leaf
- one teaspoon of thyme, dried
- one cup of Cognac
- one tablespoon of parsley, fresh, chopped

Directions:

Add one cup of flour to a plastic bag. Throw a few pieces of chicken into bag and shake to coat with flour. Melt one tablespoon of butter in the pressure cooker. Add ham and fry until it is slightly browned. Remove from the pressure cooker and set aside. Divide the chicken into three parts- melt two tablespoons of butter in pressure cooker, fry chicken in it in three batches. Remove from pressure cooker remove from heat and rinse cooker to remove residue after cooking. Add chicken and ham back into pressure cooker.

Put pressure cooker on medium heat; add the remaining ingredients except Cognac, parsley, and remaining two tablespoons of butter and flour (3 tablespoons). Stir thoroughly. Close the pressure cooker and bring to its full power over high heat. Reduce heat to medium and cook for eight minutes. Remove the pressure cooker from heat and allow to cool slowly. Open the pressure cooker and arrange chicken on a plate keep warm. From the liquid that remained after cooking, remove the fat, and save one cup. Melt butter in pressure cooker on medium heat. Add the remaining flour on low heat stirring with a whisk for about four minutes. Remove from heat and while still stirring gradually add saved liquid. Put pressure cooker over medium heat. Continue to stir until sauce thickens. Heat Cognac in a saucepan. Set it on fire; pour the burning Cognac into the sauce. Stir and pour sauce over chicken and serve warm.

25. Ginger Chicken

Total Time Needed: 12 minutes

Ingredients:

- half of a chicken cut into two portions
- one inch of ginger, freshly grated
- one teaspoon of garlic, minced
- one shallot with chives, peeled and sliced
- one lemon, cut into thin slices
- two teaspoons of black pepper
- one teaspoon of sea salt
- one cup of water
- one cup of dry Sherry
- one cup of soy sauce
- sesame seeds for garnish

Directions:

Rub the chicken with the garlic and ginger. Pour soy sauce, water, and Sherry into the pressure cooker, then put in the inset. Put the chicken on the inset and sprinkle with salt and pepper. Place the onion and lemon slices on the chicken. Close the pressure cooker and bring it to its full power over high heat. Reduce the heat to medium and cook for an additional 10 minutes. Remove the pressure cooker from the heat and leave to cool slowly. Open the pressure cooker and take out the chicken and set aside. Remove the insert and continue to cook sauce adding shallots, stirring for a few minutes. Then add chicken back into pot and mix well. Make sure to remove the onion and lemon slices from your chicken before you put it back in pot with sauce. Stir and heat for a few minutes put on serving plates, sprinkle with sesame seeds and chives serve it warm.

Chapter 6- Pressure Cooker Vegetable

26. Stuffed Tomatoes

Total Time Needed: 15 minutes

Ingredients:

- four fresh medium sized tomatoes
- one tablespoon of organic butter
- one small onion, finely chopped
- one teaspoon of pepper
- one teaspoon of salt
- one cup of low-fat cottage cheese
- one slice of whole wheat bread, crumbled
- one cup of mushrooms, finely chopped
- two tablespoons of celery, finely chopped
- one cup of water
- one tablespoon of parsley, fresh, chopped
- one teaspoon of cumin

Directions:

Cut the tomatoes stem to bottom, cutting the tip off each, then put aside. Using a spoon hollow out the tomatoes and put the pulp into a saucepan. Melt butter, add onion, and celery and stir-fry until the onion gets glossy. Add mushrooms. Cook until the liquid evaporates, stirring occasionally. Add all the other ingredients except for water. Divide into four portions and fill the tomatoes with it. Cover with the cut top of tomatoes. Pour the water into the pressure cooker, place the inset into the pressure cooker. Place the tomatoes on the insert. Close the pressure cooker and bring to full power over high heat. Immediately remove the pressure cooker from the heat and reduce the pressure placing the cooker in about two inches of water in sink for about two minutes. Open the pressure cooker and serve warm.

27. Stuffed Green Peppers

Total Time Needed: 15 minutes

Ingredients:

- four green peppers
- one cup of water

Vegetarian filling:

- two cups of cheddar cheese, grated
- one teaspoon of black pepper
- one teaspoon of sea salt
- four tablespoons of tomato, finely chopped, and peeled
- one quarter of a red onion, grated
- one cup of long grain rice, boiled

Or Tuna filling:

- one can of tuna, drained, in pieces
- two cups of cheddar cheese, grated
- one teaspoon of black pepper
- one teaspoon of sea salt
- one cup of mushrooms, finely chopped
- one quarter of a red onion, grated
- one cup of long grain rice, boiled

Directions:

Cut a hole around the tail of the peppers and remove the seed core from them gently. Rinse the core of peppers out to remove remaining seeds. Mix all of your filling ingredients in a bowl (vegetarian or tuna) except for one-cup of cheese. Divide your filling into four portions and stuff each pepper with the filling, knead filling well. Pour water into the pressure cooker and place the inset into it. Place your peppers onto the inset. Close the pressure cooker and bring to full power over high heat. Reduce heat to medium and cook for one minute. Remove the pressure cooker from the heat, reduce the pressure by placing pot into two inches of water in the sink for about two minutes. Open the pressure cooker and remove the peppers. Sprinkle the remaining cheese on top of the peppers. Bake the peppers in the oven for five minutes or until the cheese melts, serve warm.

28. Spicy Paneer

Total Time Needed: 10 minutes

Ingredients:

- one red onion, grated
- twelve ounces of green peas
- seven ounces of Paneer cheese, cubed
- a pinch of turmeric
- a few coriander leaves, chopped for garnish
- sea salt to taste
- four tablespoons of coconut oil
- one teaspoon of cumin
- one teaspoon of coriander powder
- one teaspoon of chili powder
- one inch of ginger, chopped
- two medium tomatoes, chopped

Directions:

In a saucepan lightly fry the Paneer cheese. In the pressure cooker, preheat the oil and slightly brown the onion. Add the ginger and one cup of water then add the tomatoes, spices, and fry until the fat separates. Add peas and fry for two minutes then pour in half a cup of water. Close the lid of pressure cooker and bring to full power over high heat. Reduce the heat to medium and cook for three minutes. Remove the pressure cooker and release the steam. Open and add the Paneer cheese, then cook for another two minutes. Serve sprinkled with chopped coriander leaves.

29. Curry

Total Time Needed: 10 minutes

Ingredients:

- one large red onion, grated
- seven ounces of peas, hulled
- two red potatoes, peeled, and cubed
- one large pinch of turmeric
- one teaspoon of ground cumin
- one teaspoon of ground coriander
- one teaspoon of chili powder
- one inch of ginger, chopped
- one large tomato, chopped
- three tablespoons of coconut oil
- sea salt to taste
- coriander leaves, as garnish

Directions:

Preheat your oil in the pressure cooker and then add onions, ginger, add tomato after five minutes add the peas, potatoes, spices, and salt. Stir-fry for three minutes. Add two cups of water. Close the pressure cooker bringing to full power over high heat. Reduce the heat to medium and cook for three minutes.

Remove the pressure cooker from the heat and leave to cool slowly. Serve with coriander leaves as a garnish.

30. Egg, Corn Soup

Total Time Needed: 40 minutes

Ingredients:

- four fresh corn cobs
- one stalk of celery, chopped
- one red pepper, thinly sliced
- two tablespoons of cornstarch
- two eggs, soaked in boiling water for a moment
- salt and pepper to taste
- one teaspoon of Worcestershire sauce
- one teaspoon of peanut oil
- two chives, chopped for garnishing

Directions:

Mix your cornstarch in a little bit of water. In the pressure cooker boil 500 ml of water; add the corncobs, red pepper, celery, and salt and pepper. Close the pressure cooker and bring to full power over high heat. Reduce the heat to medium and cook for 15 minutes. Remove the pressure cooker from the heat and cool slowly. Open pressure cooker and strain the broth into a separate pot. Cut the kernels of corn from the cobs and add to the broth put on low heat. Add and mix cornstarch and water, Worcestershire sauce, peanut oil. Stir thoroughly. Cook for another 15 minutes on low heat. At the end add the eggs, and beat them with a fork. Serve warm with chili sauce and soy sauce. Then sprinkle chopped chives on top of soup for garnish.

Date & Apple Pudding

Total Time Needed: one hour

Ingredients:

- one cup of walnuts, chopped
- one cup of dates, chopped
- one large apple, peeled, and sliced
- one cup plus one teaspoon of sugar
- three cups of almond flour
- one teaspoon of allspice
- one teaspoon of cinnamon
- one teaspoon of nutmeg
- two eggs
- three cups of water
- two tablespoons of coconut oil
- one teaspoon of baking powder

Directions:

Mix the dates with apple, nuts and one cup of sugar (sugar can be replaced by sugar substitute such as Stevia). Mix flour, baking soda, salt, spice blend, cinnamon, nutmeg, then add to fruits and mix well. In a separate bowl, beat the eggs with oil, add to the other ingredients and mix well. Put the mixture into mold greased with butter, sprinkle with remaining sugar, and tightly cover with aluminum foil. Pour three cups of water into the pressure cooker, put in the inset and place the mold on top of it. Close the pressure cooker, but do not put the vent weight on. Cook over high heat until the valve begins to emit steam. Reduce the heat and be sure the steam is still escaping from the vent; cook for 15 minutes. After this apply weight valve and bring to full power boiling over high heat. Reduce heat to medium and cook for 40 minutes. Remove the pressure cooker from the heat and leave to cool slowly. Open the pressure cooker and remove the mold and gently remove the pudding from the mold using a knife. Put a plate on mold then turn upside down and shake gently to get the pudding out of mold. Serve warm or chilled.

Lemon Creme

Total Time Needed: 10 minutes

Ingredients:

- one egg
- one cup of milk
- one tablespoon of sugar or sugar replacement such as Stevia
- one teaspoon of lemon peel, grated
- one teaspoon of lemon juice
- tiny pinch of salt
- three cups of water
- whipped cream for garnish

Directions:

Bring the milk to boil and cool down. In a bowl whisk the eggs with the sugar, peel, and lemon juice as well as the salt. Mix well and slowly add the milk. Heat two heat resistant molds with butter and pour the cream into them. Cover tightly with aluminum foil. Pour water into the pressure cooker, put in the inset, and arrange the molds on top of it. Close the pressure cooker lid and bring to full power over high heat. Reduce heat to medium and cook for five minutes. Remove from heat and place in cold water about two inches for two minutes in sink. Remove the lid from pressure cooker and take out molds and remove the foil. Put aside to cool, then put into the fridge to chill, add spoonful of whipped cream just before serving, then enjoy!

Carrot Halva

Total Time Needed: five minutes

Ingredients:

- 15 ounces of carrots, grated
- seven ounces of condensed unsweetened milk
- four ounces of sugar or sugar substitute such as Stevia
- ten almonds, peeled
- one ounce of ghee
- one teaspoon of cardamom powder

Directions:

Put the carrot into the pressure cooker. Close the pressure cooker and bring to full power over high heat. Open immediately after the release of the accumulated steam. Add milk, ghee, and sugar. Fry until the carrots are slightly browned. Serve Sprinkled with chopped almonds and cardamom.

Chocolate Souffle

Total Time Needed: 20 minutes

Ingredients:

- one ounce of butter
- five eggs
- five fluid ounces of milk
- four ounces of chocolate
- five drops of vanilla essence
- one teaspoon of sugar powder
- two tablespoons of almond flour

Directions:

Grease your pudding mold with non-stick cooking spray. Break the chocolate and melt boiling milk. Cool down. In a saucepan melt the butter, add flour, and fry for a few minutes. Add the milk with chocolate and stir until it thickens. Let it cool down for a bit, add one egg yolk at a time. Add vanilla essence and sugar. At the end, mix gently with rigidly beaten egg whites. Transfer to mold and cover with greased baking paper. Pour six ounces of water into the pressure cooker and put in the inset and place the mold on top of it. Close the pressure cooker and bring to full power over high heat. Reduce the heat to medium and cook for 15 minutes.

Remove the pressure cooker from the heat and leave to cool slowly. Open the pressure cooker and remove the paper, put and inverted plate on the mold, turn it upside down, gently shake. Garnish top with powdered sugar and enjoy!

Apple Walnut Bread Desert

Total Time Needed: 30 minutes

Ingredients:

- eight ounces of stale bread
- half a cup of water
- half a cup of sugar or sugar substitute such as Stevia
- two tablespoons of rum
- 500 grams of apples, peeled, cores removed, seeded
- powdered sugar for garnish
- two tablespoons of walnuts, crushed

Directions:

Grease the non-perforated inset with butter and arrange bread loafs on it; cover the bread with apple slices, walnuts, drizzle with sugar and cinnamon and tiny bits of butter, then place the next layer of bread, apples etc., until you run out of ingredients. Press well and then drizzle with water and rum. Cover with a piece of baking paper and then with a tiny plate. Put the inset into pressure cooker. Make sure to pour two cups of water at the bottom of the pressure cooker. Close the pressure cooker and come to full power over high heat. Reduce heat to medium and cook for 25 minutes. Remove the pressure cooker from heat and allow to cool slowly. Sprinkle top of apple, cake, bread with powdered sugar for garnish and enjoy!

Conclusion

I hope you will have as much fun trying this collection of recipes as I did in putting them together. Baking and preparing meals is a great way to spend some time with your loved ones such as your children. Teaching them how to prepare meals is a lesson that is not only fun but also very yummy! Helping you to prepare a meal will build up your child's self-confidence and yours when you both get the thumbs up for a tasty meal that you prepared together! I wish you great fun and enjoyment (especially for your taste buds) in preparing and enjoying these tasty pressure cooker recipes!

Thanks again for downloading my book I would greatly appreciate it if you would be so kind as to leave a small review of my book—it would help me out a lot—I hope you will continue to read my collection of cookbooks!

Part 2

Introduction

Whether you want to whip up succulent beef dishes, tender pork roasts, perfectly cooked chicken and savory seafood as well as perfect side dishes to serve with your easy to make entrees, you can do it all and do so in minutes.

Explore the diverse options that you have using this handy kitchen staple.

Pressure Cooking

The process behind pressure cooking is simple. Food is cooked in an airtight pot, which does not allow air or liquid to be released below a pre-determined pressure. This results in food that is cooked faster versus conventional cooking methods via a saturated steam of flavors that adds to the richness of the recipes that you are creating.

While best suited for any food that requires steam or liquids for cooking, almost anything can be cooked using a pressure cooker. Don't let the numerous parts of this contraption intimidate you—once you get the hang of it, the process is simple.

A pressure cooker is typically made of a steel or aluminum body with handles, a lid with a slider or locking device and a gasket that is completely airtight and liquid proof. It also comes equipped with a steam vent that maintains the pot's pressure level and a steamer basket, trivet and metal divider.

Here are the main advantages of using a pressure cooker:
- Food cooks faster versus traditional cooking methods.
- Requires less water than boiling, again, adding to the efficiency of cooking.
- Vitamins and minerals are easily absorbed into the ingredients and are preserved very well.
- It is convenient to use.
- A brilliant time and energy saver.

Pressure cooking tips and tricks

Whether you're an expert cook who has used the pressure cooker to create sumptuous meals or are new to the concept, it wouldn't hurt to keep the following in mind when using a pressure cooker:

- While aluminum made pots for pressure cookers are available now, the material tends to react with acidic food, which results in flavor changes. It is also less durable than its steel counterparts. Opt for the heavy stainless steel pots with copper-clad bottoms that distribute heat more evenly instead.

- Pressure cooking will require liquid. It is not advisable for roasting or frying.

- Thick sauces do not have enough liquid to create steam required for cooking. As such, it usually ends up burning into the bottom of the pot when exposed to too much heat. If sauce requires thickening, do so before adding into the pressure cooker.

- Frozen ingredients are not advisable to be cooked inside a pressure cooker. This will extend cooking time unnecessarily and inevitably lead to burning your ingredients.

- You can improve the flavor of your meals by preheating your oils or butter in an open pressure cooker.

- Brown meat before securing the lid of your pressure cooker.

- Remember that there are different ways to open your pressure cooker. Do not simply pop the lid off as this might spray hot steam all over:

- Cold water release is the fastest way to release pressure, which requires you to place slow cold tap water to run over the edge of the lid, while avoiding the steam vent and valves. Do not immerse the pressure cooker under water.

- Manual or quick release is the normal method used that requires to release vapor by removing the valve, turning a knob or in electric pressure cookers, pushing a button. This is required for multiple ingredient recipes where meat and vegetables are combined in one pot.

- The natural release method means pressure drops slowly and without prompting. This normally takes about 10 to 15 minutes.

Chicken

Chicken in Honeyed Vinaigrette

Prep Time: 30 minutes
Servings: 4

Ingredients:

1 3/4 lbs. chicken thighs, deboned and skinned
3 cloves garlic, crushed and minced
1 tsp. dried basil
1/2 cup soy sauce
1/2 cup balsamic vinaigrette
1/3 cup honey
1/3 cup olive oil

Directions:

1. Heat oil in a pressure cooker over medium high heat.
2. Add chicken into the pot and brown on all sides.
3. In a separate bowl, whisk all remaining ingredients together and pour over the chicken.
4. Cover and secure lid. Cook for 10-15 minutes under high pressure or until meat is tender.

5. Drizzle chicken with drippings.

BBQ Chicken

Prep Time: 30 minutes
Servings: 4-6

Ingredients:

1/2 cup cola soft drink
1/3 cup ketchup
1/4 cup brown sugar
2 tbsps. apple cider vinegar
2 tbsps. bourbon
1 lemon, sliced
2 tsps. salt
1/2 tsp. pepper
1 1/2 tsps. paprika
1/2 tsp. garlic powder
3 1/4 lbs. whole chicken
3 tbsps. olive oil

Directions:

1. Whisk all ingredients together, except the chicken and olive oil. Set aside.
2. Heat oil in a pressure cooker and brown on all sides. Remove.

3. Place rack carefully in the middle of the pot and pour sauce set aside in step 1.
4. Cover and secure lid; bring up to pressure. Cook for 20-25 minutes.

Spicy Lime Chicken Strips

Prep Time: 6-7 hours
Servings: 2-4

Ingredients:

2 1/2 lbs. chicken drumsticks
1 tbsp. brown sugar
1 tbsp. all spice
1 tsp. cinnamon
1/2 tsp. cayenne pepper
2 tsps. salt
3 limes, juiced
3 tbsps. olive oil

Directions:

1. Whisk all ingredients together, except of the chicken.
2. Heat oil in pressure cooker over medium heat and brown chicken on all sides.
3. Pour sauce over chicken and cover the pot.
4. Secure lid and bring pressure up to high. Cook for 8-10 minutes.

Sour Cream Chicken

Prep Time: 30 minutes
Servings: 2

Ingredients:

1 tbsp. vegetable oil
4 lbs. chicken leg quarters, skinned
1 small onion, finely chopped
2 tsp. hot paprika, preferably Hungarian
1/2 cup chicken broth
1 medium Tomato, peeled and coarsely chopped
1 tsp. salt
1/2 cup sour cream

Directions:

1. Heat oil over high heat in the pressure cooker and brown chicken pieces on all sides then set aside.
2. Add onion, broth and paprika and stir mixture in the pot.
3. Place chicken back into the pot and add tomatoes and season with salt.
4. Cover and secure lid. Bring pressure up to high and cook for 4-5 minutes.

5. Lower heat to medium and cook for an additional 7 minutes.
6. Once ready, remove chicken and take 1/4 cup of the drippings. Whisk with sour cream until smooth and pour over chicken.

Herbed Chicken

Prep Time: 20 minutes
Servings: 6-8

Ingredients:

4 lbs. chicken breasts
1 1/2 tsps. salt
1 tsp. black pepper
2 tsps. herbes de provence
1 tsp. paprika
8 cherry tomatoes, halved
1/2 cup olive oil

Directions:

1. Whisk oil with herbs and seasonings.
2. Place in a pressure cooker over medium heat and brown chicken breasts on all sides.
3. Once ready, arrange all pieces in the pot in one layer and top with tomatoes.
4. Cover and turn pressure up to high. Cook for 8-10 minutes.

Beef

Hearty Beef Ribs

Prep Time: 20 minutes
Servings: 6

Ingredients:

1/4 cup cider vinegar
2 tbsps. Worcestershire sauce
1 onion, sliced
3 lbs. beef ribs, deboned
16 oz. picante sauce
1/2 cup butter
3 tbsps. olive oil

Directions:

1. Place olive oil and butter in a pressure cooker and brown beef ribs on all sides.
2. Whisk all remaining ingredients together and pour over ribs.
3. Cover and turn pressure up to high. Cook for 15 minutes.

Citrus and Ginger Beef

Prep Time: 40 minutes
Servings: 4-6

Ingredients:

1 1/2 lbs. beef rounds, sliced into strips
1/4 cup soy sauce
2 tsps. ground ginger
3 tbsps. honey
1/2 cup lemon juice
6 green onions, sliced
3 tbsps. olive oil

Directions:

1. Heat olive oil in pressure cooker and sear beef rounds quickly on each side.
2. Whisk all remaining ingredients together and pour over beef.
3. Cover and raise pressure to high. Cook for 20-25 minutes.

Classic Beef and Mushroom

Prep Time: 40 minutes
Servings: 6-8

Ingredients:

1 lb. cubed beef
1 10 3/4 oz. condensed mushroom soup
1/2 cup onion (chopped)
1 tbsp. Worcestershire sauce
1 cup button mushrooms, halved
4 oz. cream cheese, softened
1 tbsp. paprika
3 tbsps. olive oil

Directions:

1. Heat olive oil in a pressure cooker and quickly brown cubed beef in the pot.
2. Whisk Worcestershire sauce with cream cheese, paprika and mushroom soup. Add into pot and mix well with beef.
3. Top with button mushrooms and onions.
4. Cover and turn pressure up to high. Cook for 20-25 minutes.

Pot Roast and Buttered Potatoes

Prep Time: 45 minutes
Servings: 6

Ingredients:

1 cup butter, softened
1/2 cup parsley, chopped finely
4 tbsps. olive oil
1 oz. dry onion soup and recipe mix
1/2 cup Worcestershire sauce
6 small red potatoes, sliced in half
3 1/4 lbs. boneless beef bottom round roast

Directions:

1. Heat oil in a pressure cooker and brown roast on all sides. Set roast aside.
2. Place a rack in the middle of your pot and place roast on top.
3. Whisk onion soup mix with Worcestershire sauce and pour over roast.

4. Mash butter with parsley in a bowl and toss until potatoes are well coated. Arrange potatoes around the roast.
5. Cover and bring pressure up to high. Cook for 20-25 minutes.

Pineapple Beef Teriyaki

Prep Time: 25 minutes
Servings: 2-4

Ingredients:

2 lbs. stew beef
1 jar teriyaki sauce
1 cup pineapple tidbits
2 tbsps. sesame oil
2 tbsps. sesame seeds

Directions:

1. Heat sesame oil over medium heat in a pressure cooker.
2. Sear beef quickly and pour teriyaki sauce over it.
3. Add pineapple tidbits and sprinkle with sesame seeds.
4. Cover and cook on high for 20 minutes.

Pork

Home-cooked Sweet Ham

Prep Time: 20 minutes
Servings: 6-8

Ingredients:

6 lbs. ham, with bone
1/4 cup apple cider vinegar
1/4 cup honey
1/4 cup butter, melted
1 tsp. gluten Worcestershire sauce
1 tbsp. brown sugar
2 tsps. thyme

Directions:

1. Combine flavorings and spices in a bowl and whisk together.
2. Place ham inside a pressure cooker and pour over the ham.
3. Cover and cook on high for 20 minutes.
4. Glaze ham using drippings before carving.

Soy and Ginger Pork Chops

Prep Time: 25 minutes
Servings: 6

Ingredients:

6 pork chops, deboned
1/4 cup brown sugar
1 tsp. ground ginger
1/2 cup soy sauce
2 cloves crushed garlic
2 tbsps. sesame oil
Salt
Pepper

Directions:

1. Heat sesame oil over medium heat and brown chops on both sides.
2. Whisk remaining ingredients together and pour over chops.
3. Cover and cook on high for 15 to 20 minutes.

Adobo Pork Stew

Prep Time: 30 minutes
Servings: 4-6

Ingredients:

1 3/4 lbs. pork ribs, deboned
1 onion, sliced
1 tbsp. garlic, minced
1 tbsp. paprika
2 tsps. fresh oregano
1 chile, minced
1/3 cup soy sauce
2 cups canned chopped tomatoes (keep sauce/ juices)
1 tbsp. red wine vinegar
3 tbsps. olive oil

Directions:

1. Heat olive oil in the pressure cooker over medium to high heat.
2. Add garlic and brown meat on all sides.
3. Whisk together all remaining ingredients and pour over pork.
4. Cover and cook on high for 20 minutes.

Pork Roast

Prep Time: 60 minutes
Servings: 8-10

Ingredients:

1 onion, sliced into rings
3 1/2 lbs. pork roast
2 tbsps. brown sugar
1 tbsp. ground coriander
1 tbsp. paprika
1 tsp. ground cumin
1 tsp. anise seeds
1 tsp. kosher salt
1/2 tsp. black pepper
2 tbsps. olive oil

Directions:

1. Heat oil in a pressure cooker.
2. Rub roast with spices and seasonings. Brown in hot oil on all sides.
3. Add onion rings on top.
4. Cover and cook on high for 40 minutes.

Cranberry Pork Cutlets

Prep Time: 30 minutes
Servings: 6-8

Ingredients:

16 oz. cranberry sauce
1/3 cup French salad dressing
1 onion, sliced thinly
3 lbs. boneless pork loin roast, sliced thickly
1/3 cup olive oil

Directions:

1. Heat oil in a pressure cooker and brown pork slices.
2. Whisk salad dressing in cranberry sauce and pour over pork.
3. Top with onions.
4. Cover and cook on high for 20-25 minutes.

Seafood

Seafood Stew

Prep Time: 10 minutes
Servings: 4

Ingredients:

2 cups chicken broth
1/2 cup white wine
1 cup brown rice, uncooked
1 can stewed tomatoes
1/2 can black beans, drained
1/2 onion, chopped
1/2 head garlic, chopped
3 chopped celery, chopped
1 green pepper
1 red pepper
1 cup white corn, kernels
2 cups shrimp, cooked
1/2 lb. sausages, chopped

Directions:

1. Combine all ingredients in a pressure cooker over medium high heat.
2. Cover and bring pressure up to high. Cook for 5-7 minutes.

Snapper in Sesame Soy Sauce

Prep Time: 20 minutes
Servings: 4-6

Ingredients:

6 oz. snapper fillets
Ground black pepper
2 1/2 tsps. soy sauce
1 1/2 tsps. lemon juice
1 1/2 tsps. brown sugar
1 tsp. honey
1 tsp. toasted sesame seeds
1 cup chicken broth
2 tbsps. sesame oil

Directions:

1. Heat sesame oil in pressure cooker.
2. Whisk together soy sauce, lemon juice, sugar, honey and sesame seeds
3. Add salmon fillets, chicken stock and pour sauce over it.
4. Cover and cook for 6 minutes.

Coconut Halibut Stew

Prep Time: 15 minutes
Servings: 1

Ingredients:

8 oz. halibut fillets
1/2 tsp. salt
1/2 tsp. black pepper
1 1/2 cups light coconut milk
1/2 cup vegetable stock
1 cup green onions, chopped

Directions:

1. Combine coconut milk, vegetable stock, salt, pepper and onions in a pressure cooker over medium heat.
2. Add fish fillets as it simmers.
3. Cover and cook for 4-6 minutes.

Celery and Shrimp Stew

Prep Time: 15 minutes
Servings: 1

Ingredients:

1 1/2 lb. shrimp, peeled and deveined
1 1/2 oz. cream of celery soup
1 1/2 cups celery, chopped
2 1 1/2 oz. milk
2 tbsps. butter
1 tsp. Old Bay Seasoning
1/4 tsp. salt
1/4 tsp. pepper

Directions:

1. Combine cream of celery, celery, milk, butter and seasonings in a pressure cooker over medium heat.
2. Allow mixture to simmer and add shrimp.
3. Cover and cook for 1-2 minutes on low.

Shrimp Marinara with Spaghetti

Prep Time: 4 hours
Servings: 6

Ingredients:

1 can tomatoes, diced and juices set aside
1 can tomato paste
1/2 to 1 cup water
2 garlic cloves, minced
2 tbsps. fresh parsley, minced
1 tsp. salt
1 tsp. oregano
1/2 tsp. basil
1/4 tsp. pepper
1 lb. shrimp, peeled and deveined
1 lb. spaghetti noodles, cooked and drained
Shredded Parmesan cheese

Directions:

1. Add tomatoes, tomato paste, water with herbs and seasonings in a pressure cooker over medium heat.
2. Let mixture simmer and add shrimp.
3. Cover and cook for 1-2 minutes.
4. Serve on top of cooked spaghetti noodles and a sprinkle of parmesan cheese.

Snacks and Starters

Garlic and Herb Creamy Potatoes

Prep Time: 10 minutes
Servings: 6-8

Ingredients:

3 large potatoes, peeled and cubed
1 cup chicken broth
1 cup warm skim milk
2 tbsps. olive oil
1 tbsp. minced thyme
1/2 tsp. garlic powder
1/2 tsp. dried rosemary, crushed
1/2 tsp. salt
1/4 tsp. pepper
3 cloves of garlic, minced

Directions:

1. Combine potatoes, garlic and broth in a pressure cooker.
2. Close and cook on high for 6 minutes.

3. Open and pour milk and olive oil. Use a hand mixer to blend until mixture if fluffy.
4. Add herbs and season with salt and pepper. Mix well.

Babaganoush and Crackers

Prep Time: 3 hours
Servings: 6-8

Ingredients:

2 lbs. eggplant, cut into large cubes
1/4 cup olive oil
1 tsp. salt
1/2 cup water
3-4 cloves garlic, minced
1 clove, crushed
1/4 cup lemon juice
1 tbsp. tahini
1 bunch of thyme
Olive oil
3 black gourmet salt-cured olives
1 pack herb crackers

Directions:

1. Cover bottom of a pressure cooker with eggplant cubes. Drizzle with olive oil and brown quickly in the pot.
2. Add crushed garlic and cover. Cook for 3 minutes on high.

3. Open lid and add tahini, lemon juice and minced garlic. Use hand mixer to blend all ingredients together.
4. Serve topped with a sprinkle of thyme, olives and olive oil with crackers on the side.

Buttered Baby Carrots

Prep Time: 5 minutes
Servings: 8-10

Ingredients:

3 tablespoon butter
1 teaspoon lemon juice
1 tablespoon minced parsley
1 pound baby carrots
Salt to taste

Directions:

1. Melt butter in a pressure cooker over medium heat and add lemon juice. Whisk together.
2. Add carrots and parsley. Season well and cover.
3. Cook on high for 3-5 minutes.

Baby Rosemary Potatoes

Prep Time: 10 minutes
Servings: 6

Ingredients:

5 tablespoon butter
2 pounds baby potatoes
1 sprig rosemary
3 garlic cloves (outer skin on)
1/2 cup stock
Salt and pepper

Directions:

1. Melt butter and garlic in a pressure cooker over medium heat.
2. Toss potatoes in and allow butter to coat the potatoes.
3. Add rosemary and pour stock in. Season well.
4. Cover and cook for 5 minutes on high.

Tomato and Green Beans

Prep Time: 15 minutes
Servings: 1

Ingredients:

1 tablespoon olive oil
1 garlic clove, crushed
2 cups of fresh cherry tomatoes
1 pound green beans, trimmed
2 pinches salt
1 sprig basil

Directions:

1. Heat oil in a pressure cooker over medium heat.
2. Add garlic cloves and toss in tomatoes and greens.
3. Add basil and season with salt.
4. Cover and cook for 8-12 minutes on high.

Baked Beans

Prep Time: 35 minutes
Servings: 1

Ingredients:

1 1/4 cups dried navy beans, about 1/2 pound
1 small onion, finely chopped
1/4 pound sliced bacon, cut crosswise into 1/2-inch strips
1/4 cup ketchup
2 tablespoons light brown sugar
2 tablespoons molasses
1 tablespoon prepared mustard
1 tablespoon vegetable oil
3/4 teaspoon salt
1/2 teaspoon pepper
5 cups water, divided

Directions:

1. Pour 4 cups of water and beans in a pressure cooker over high heat. Cover and cook for 3 minutes.
2. Drain and place in a bowl with onions, bacon, sugar, ketchup, molasses, oil, salt, pepper, mustard and remaining water.

3. Pour mixture back into the pot and cook for 20-25 minutes.

Spicy Chicken Spread

Prep Time: 15 minutes
Servings: 6

Ingredients:

2 packages of cream cheese
2-3 cans of shredded chicken breast in water
10 oz. ranch dressing
1/2 bottle Buffalo Sauce
1 cup shredded cheddar cheese

Directions:

1. Combine all ingredients in a pressure cooker over medium heat.
2. Mix well and cover.
3. Cook on low for 12 minutes.

Hearty Bowl of Chili

Prep Time: 15 minutes
Servings: 6

Ingredients:

2 1/2 lbs. beef chuck roast
15 oz. can taco sauce
3/4 cup butter
1 cup beef broth
1 onion, sliced
3 garlic cloves, minced
1 tsp. salt
1/2 tsp. crushed red pepper

Directions:

1. Combine all ingredients in a slow cooker.
2. Cover and cook on high for 10-12 minutes.

Sour Cream Potatoes and Chives

Prep Time: 10 minutes
Servings: 4

Ingredients:

4 medium russet potatoes, chopped
1 cup vegetable broth
2 cups sour cream
Fresh chives, minced
2 cups shredded cheese of choice

Directions:

1. Place potatoes in a pressure cooker and add broth.
2. Cover and cook on high for 6-8 minutes.
3. Combine sour cream and chives and whisk together.
4. Serve potatoes with a heaping of sour cream and a sprinkle of cheese.

Chips n' Dip

Prep Time: 15 minutes
Servings: 4

Ingredients:

1 can chopped green chili's
1 cup salsa
1 teaspoon oregano
1/2 teaspoon ground cumin
1/2 teaspoon garlic powder
2 cans creamy three cheese cooking sauce
1/2 cup chopped cilantro
1 bag tortilla chips of choice

Directions:

1. Combine salsa, cheese sauce with herbs and seasonings and chili's.
2. Stir well and cover. Cook on high for 8-10 minutes.
3. Serve with chips on the side.

PORK and BEEF

Pork Chops

Servings: 6-8
Total Time: 25 Minutes
Ingredients:
- 8 Center Cut Pork Chops
- 1 Cup of Water
- 3 Tablespoons of Steak Sauce &/or 3 Tablespoons of Worcestershire Sauce
- ¼ Cup of Butter
- 1 Onion
- 4-6 Potatoes- Diced
- Pepper & Salt to Taste
- Optional: Carrot

Directions:
1. Peel, chunk, and portion potatoes, carrots, and onion to prepare for recipe
2. Place butter, salt and pepper in a pan (Not Covered) Brown Pork Chops on both sides by using tongs.
3. Take Pork Chops out of Pan.
4. Add potatoes, carrots, and onions to pan. Place Pork Chops on top of the vegetables.
5. Add 1 Cup of Water and 3 Tablespoons of Steak Sauce.

6. Place Lid. Bring Pressure Cooker on High for 15 minutes.

Creamy Pork Chops

Serves: 3-6
Total Time: 30 minutes
Ingredients:
- 6 Pork Chops
- 1 ½ Cups of Water
- 1 10 1/2oz Can of Cream of Mushroom Soup
- 1 ½ Cups of Sour Cream
- 2-3 Tablespoons of Oil
- 2 Teaspoons of Chicken Bouillon Powder
- 1 Tablespoon of Chopped Fresh Parsley
- Pepper to Taste

Directions:
1. Heat Oil over medium heat until hot in Pressure Cooker
2. Brown Pork Chops on both sides. Remove from pan.
3. Add the chicken bouillon powder and water to the pressure cooker.
4. Place browned Pork Chops back into pan.
5. Place lid on cooker. Cook for 8 minutes before turning off heat.
6. After removing Pork Chops, add Cream of Mushroom Soup over medium heat.
7. Whisk Sour Cream in over LOW heat.
8. Stir in Parsley last.

9. Next, pour sauce over Pork Chops and enjoy your meal!

Spanish Braised Pork

Servings: 8

Total Time: 1 Hour 15 Minutes

Ingredients:
- 5 pounds of Pork Romp- ½ inch cubes
- ¼ Cup of Minced Onion
- 2 Cups of Red Wine
- 2 Tablespoons of Olive Oil
- 2 Cups of Chicken Stock
- ½ Cup of Lemon Juice
- ¼ Cup of Garlic Powder
- 1 Tablespoon of Paprika

Directions:
1. In your Pressure Cooker: Place Pork, minced onion, olive oil, paprika, and garlic powder evenly.
2. Next, add Chicken stock, lemon juice, and red wine. Be sure it covers the meat completely. If not, add more chicken stock to recipe.
3. Bring pressure cooker to high heat for a few minutes
4. Turn Heat down to maintain pressure in cooker and cook for 45 minutes.

5. After allowed time, leave meal in cooker for 15 minutes before releasing pressure.

Pork Chop Suey

Servings: 6-8
Total Time: 2 Hours 30 Minutes
Ingredients:
- 5-6 Pork Steaks
- 8-10 White Mushrooms, preferably Fresh.
- 1 Yellow Onion
- 3 Stalks of Celery
- 2 14 oz Cans of Undrained Bean Sprouts
- ½ Cup of Water
- 1 Tablespoon of Vegetable Oil
- 1/3 Cup of Soy Sauce
- 1 14 oz. can of Chicken Broth
- 2 Tablespoons of Butter
- 4 Tablespoons of Molasses
- 2 Tablespoons of Cornstarch

Directions:
1. For preparation:
   Cut Pork into ½ inch cubes
Slice Celery, Onion, Mushrooms into small, thin slices
Mix 2 Tablespoons of Cornstarch into ½ Cup of Water

2. Heat the Oil in Pressure Cooker then add butter until the mix begins to bubble.
3. Add ½ inch pork cubes and brown on all sides
4. Next, add your chopped celery, onion, and mushrooms.
5. Cook mixture over medium heat while stirring until they are tender.
6. Once tender, add 1/3 cup of soy sauce, bean sprouts, and the 14 oz. can of chicken broth to the mix.
7. Add the 4 tablespoons of molasses next and stir
8. Cover pot and allow mixture to simmer for at least one hour.
9. While using pressure cooker: Bring to slow rocking pressure and cook for 10 minutes.
10. Allow 20 minutes of simmering by removing cover and letting cool down.
11. Once Pork is Tender, mix the corn starch water into pot.
12. Allow mixture to cook for 15 minutes
13. This can be served over Pasta or Rice. Enjoy!

Beer Braised Ribs

Servings: 4
Total Time: 45 minutes
Ingredients:
- 4 pounds of pork rib
- 12-ounce bottle of beer
- 1 cup of water
- 1 cup of barbecue sauce
- 2 tablespoons of cider vinegar

Directions:
1. Place beer, vinegar, and water into your pressure cooker together.
2. Place ribs into the mixture. Be sure they are not stacked on top of one another.
3. Heat pressure cooker over high heat followed by a lower heat to maintain pressure.
4. Cook ribs for 15 minutes before turning off heat and releasing the pressure.
5. Heat oven to 400 degrees and transfer ribs to baking pan. Here, brush barbecue sauce on ribs then roast until they are crisp on top.
6. After ten minutes, turn ribs over to brush barbecue sauce on that side as well. It is suggested to roast for another five minutes once the ribs have been rotated.

Beef Roll-Ups

Servings:4
Total Time: 20 Minutes

Ingredients:
- 2 Pounds of round steak beef
- 1 ½ pounds of beef bacon
- 2 ½ cups of water
- 2 teaspoons of cooking oil
- 1 package of onion soup mix
- 2 teaspoons of cornstarch
- 3 cherry tomatoes
- Optional: Parsley

Directions:
1. Prepare meal by trimming the fat from the steak/bacon and remove bones for easy cooking.
2. Next, pound the meat with a mallet and begin slicing the steak into one inch strips, four inches long.
3. In a large frying pan, begin to bake roll ups to the desired brownness
4. Once browned, place roll ups into your pressure pan.

5. Next, add the onion soup mix and 2 cups of water to the frying pan and begin to simmer for around 3 minutes.
6. Once the liquid is simmering, pour the mixture over the roll-ups in your pressure cooker.
7. Proceed to cook for 10 minutes then remove onto a warm serving dish.
8. In a bowl, combine the cornstarch and ½ cup of water.
9. Next, add the mixture to your pressure pan and simmer for three to four minutes. Stir until the mixture is thick.
10. Next, pour gravy over the roll up.
11. Garnish the meat with parsley and cherry tomatoes if desired.

Apple Cider Pork Chops

Servings: 6
Total Time: 30 minutes
Ingredients:
- 6 Pork Chops, about ¾ inches thick
- 6-12 dried apple slices
- 1 Cup of apple cider
- 2 Tablespoons of butter
- 2 Tablespoons of vegetable oil
- 2 Tablespoons of aspen mulling spices
- 2 Tablespoons of flour
- 2 Teaspoons of seasoning salt

Directions:
1. Begin by seasoning the pork chops with salt on both sides.
2. While allowing the pork chops to sit with salt, begin to hear the vegetable oil on the bottom of your pressure cooker over a medium heat.
3. Place the pork chops into the cooker and brown them on both sides. Remove onto a plate directly after.
4. Next, place a basket into the pressure cooker. Here, you will want to press one or two dried apple slicers onto the pork chops and spring with the aspen mulling spices.

5. After, place the pork chops into the basket inside your pressure cooker and sandwich the apple slices in between the pork chops.
6. Once this is done, begin to pour cider over the pork chops then secure the lid onto your pressure cooker.
7. Carefully bring your pressure cooker to high pressure over medium heat then adjust heat to maintain pressure.
8. Cook the pork chops in your pressure cooker for about 17 minutes.
9. After 17 minutes, remove your pressure cooker from the heat and allow a natural drop in pressure. This should take about ten minutes.
10. Next, remove the pork chops onto a serving platter and cover with tin foil to keep the food warm.
11. Once this is done, melt butter in a microwave and sit in the flour with a whisk. When butter and flour is mixed, microwave for another 40 seconds.
12. Last step is to pour the sauce over the pork chops and enjoy your meal!

Split Pea and Ham Soup

Servings: 6-8

Total Time: 40 minutes

Ingredients:
- 1 pound of ham
- 1 pound of dried split peas
- 1 onion, diced
- 2 celery stalks, diced
- 2 carrots, diced
- 8 cups of water
- 1 ½ teaspoons of dried thyme
- Optional: Sherry wine

Directions:
1. To begin, place the ham, dried split peas, onion, carrots, dried thyme, celery, and eight cups of water into your pressure cooker.
2. Place the lid on your pressure cooker and bring to a high pressure
3. Once this is done, cook the ingredients for about 20 minutes.
4. Once 20 minutes has passed, allow cooler to release pressure naturally.
5. Next, add salt to taste if you wish.
6. Optional: Serve the soup with a splash of Sherry if desired.

Mushroom Beef Stew

Servings: 4
Total Time: 20 minutes
Ingredients:
- 1 ½ pounds of stew meat
- 4 carrots, peeled
- 4 red potatoes
- 8-12 button mushrooms
- 1 large onion
- 1-2 beef bouillon cubes
- 10 ounces of condensed golden mushroom soup
- 10-20 ounces of water
- 1-2 teaspoons of dried parsley
- 2 tablespoons of canola oil

Directions:
1. To begin, heat the canola oil in your pressure cooker until it is simmering
2. Add the meat to the oil and stir until it is brown on all sides.
3. Once meat is browned, add the carrots, potatoes, mushrooms, onions, parsley, mushroom soup, water, and if desired: the beef bouillon.
4. Place the lid on your pressure cooker and bring to high pressure over a high heat.

5. You will want to cook the mixture for about 15 minutes.
6. Once time is passed, cool the pot immediately. Your meal is ready to serve!

Pressure Cooked Meatballs

Servings: 4
Total Time: 40 minutes

Ingredients:
- 1 pound of extra lean ground beef
- 8 ounces of ground pork
- 1 small onion, minced
- 1 slice of whole wheat bread
- 1 ½ tablespoons of dried thyme
- 1 tablespoon of dried oregano
- ½ teaspoon of salt
- ¼ cup of all-purpose flour
- 1 egg
- ½ cup of milk
- ¼ cup of butter
- ¾ can of chicken stock diluted with equal amount of water
- Salt and pepper to taste

Directions:
1. In a bowl, soak the whole wheat bread in milk until it is absorbed.
2. Using hands, mix the bread into the beef and pork
3. Next, stir in the egg, thyme, oregano, salt, and minced onion.

4. Once this is done, form ¾ inch meatballs.
5. In your pressure cooker, melt the butter over a medium-high heat then proceed to stir in the flour. Place meatballs into the sauce.
6. Lock lid of pressure cooker in place and bring to full pressure over medium-high heat. Retain pressure by lowering heat to medium-low. Cook for 10 minutes.
7. Remove from heat and release pressure quickly.
8. Last, stir in cream and simmer until the sauce becomes thick and creamy.
9. Optional: Serve meatballs over cooked egg noodles and garnish to taste.

CHICKEN

Whole Chicken

Servings: 4-6
Total Time: 30 minutes
Ingredients:
- 2 pounds of whole chicken
- 1 ½ Cups of Water or 1 ½ Cups of chicken broth
- 2 Tablespoons of Olive Oil
- Salt and Pepper to taste

Directions:
1. Prepare the two pounds of chicken by rinsing and seasoning with salt and pepper.
2. In an uncovered pressure cooker, heat the olive oil then brown chicken on all sides.
3. Remove chicken and place rack into your pressure cooker. Re-place chicken on rack then proceed to add the water and broth around the chicken.
4. Cook the chicken for 25 minutes once brought to pressure.
5. Use a quick release method to release pressure from cooker.

6. Once chicken is removed, it is suggested to pour the extra juice from the chicken and serve along the side for extra dressing.

Chicken Vegetable Soup

Servings: 4
Total Time: 28 minutes
Ingredients:
- 1 ½ Pounds of Boneless- Skinless Chicken Breasts
- 3 Chopped garlic cloves
- 1 Cup of 1-inch chunk celery
- 1 Cup of 1-inch chunk carrot
- 1 coarsely chopped Onion
- 1 Cup of chopped green onion
- 1 Cup of chopped cilantro
- 1 ½ Cups of Frozen Corn Kernels
- 1 ½ Teaspoons of Salt
- ½ Teaspoon of Pepper
- 4 Cups of Water

Directions:
1. Start preparation for meal by cutting the chicken breast into 1 inch cubes.

2. Place chicken, carrots, green onion, garlic, salt, pepper, water, celery, and cilantro into your pressure cooker.
3. Over high heat, bring cooker to pressure then reduce heat to maintain pressure.
4. Cook the mixture for 8 minutes.
5. Use quick release method to release the pressure of the cooker.
6. Remove lid then add the frozen corn kernels.
7. Heat on medium until corn is tender.

Chicken and Rice Soup

Servings: 4-6
Total Time: 30 minutes
Ingredients:
- 2 Split chicken breasts with the bone
- 4 Cups of water
- 4 Cups of chicken broth
- 3 Cups of white rice al dente
- 1 large peeled onion
- 3 peeled carrots, cut into ¼ inch rounds
- 3 pieces of celery
- 1 ½ tablespoons of salt
- 1 tablespoon of minced parsley

Directions:
1. Place chicken, broth, water, onion, and salt into your pressure cooker.
2. Cook mixture for about 10 minutes while cooker is on meat selector.
3. After 10 minutes, remove chicken and proceed to cut into chunks.
4. Next, strain broth and return to pressure cooker.
5. Add carrots and celery to the cooker.
6. Cook the mixture for 3 minutes or until tender.
7. Remove the carrots and celery from heat and release the pressure.

8. Next, add the cooked chicken with the rice and parsley.
9. Season the mixture with salt and pepper to taste.
10. Enjoy!

Cranberry Chicken

Servings: 4
Total Time: 20 minutes
Ingredients:
- 4 Boneless chicken breasts
- 1 14 oz. can of whole berry cranberry sauce
- 8 ounces of egg noodles
- 1 package of onion soup mix
- 1 cup of French dressing

Directions:
1. Prepare for your meal by mixing the French dressing, onion soup and cranberry sauce together.
2. Next, place the chicken into your pressure cooker and dress with the cranberry mixture.
3. Cook the chicken and cranberry mixture for about 12 minutes.
4. While the chicken is cooking, prepare the egg noodles on a stove according to the package directions.
5. Once the pressure is released, pour in your cooked egg noodles and your dinner is ready!

Hungarian Chicken

Servings:4

Total Time: 60 minutes

Ingredients:

- 3 ½-4pounds of chicken leg quarters
- 6 ounces of extra wide egg noodles
- 1 small onion, chopped
- 1 medium tomato, chopped
- ½ cup of chicken broth
- 1 tablespoon of vegetable oil
- ½ cup of sour cream
- 1 teaspoon of salt
- 2 teaspoons of hot paprika

Directions:

1. To begin, heat the vegetable oil over medium heat until it begins to smoke.
2. Next, add the chicken leg quarters into the oil and cook until they are golden. This should take about 4-5 minutes. Once this is done, transfer the chicken pieces onto a plate.
3. In your pressure cooker, add the chicken broth, paprika, and onion then stir mix to be sure it is evenly distributed around the pressure cooker.
4. Once step three has been completed, return the chicken on top of the mix then proceed to add tomato on top of the chicken. Do not Stir.

5. Next, you will want to sprinkle salt on top and then lock the lid into place. For 4-5 minutes, bring the pressure cooker over high heat.
6. Reduce the heat after 4-5 minutes to medium and continue to cook the chicken for another 7 minutes.
7. Remove the pressure cooker from the heat and allow the mixture to sit for another 5 minutes to allow it to finish cooking.
8. After 5 minutes, gently release any remaining pressure from the cooker before transferring the chicken to a plate.
9. In a small bowl on the side, whisk sour cream and the remaining liquid from the pot together until smooth.
10. Next, pour the sour cream mixture into your pressure cooker and return the chicken pieces in. Reheat for a moment but do not bring to a boil.
11. Last, you will want to place your warm, cooked egg noodles onto a serving platter and arrange the chicken on top of the noodles. Pour the remaining sauce over the chicken and egg noodles and your meal is complete!

Chicken Piccata

Servings: 6
Total Time: 42 minutes

Ingredients:
- 6 chicken breast halves
- 4 shallots
- 3 garlic cloves
- 1 lemon for garnish
- 1 tablespoon of potato starch
- ¼ cup of fresh parmesan cheese
- 2 teaspoons of salt
- 1 tablespoon of sherry wine
- 1 teaspoon of dried basil
- ¼ teaspoon of white pepper
- 1 cup of pimento stuffed olives
- 1 cup of sour cream
- ½ cup of flour
- ¾ cup of chicken broth
- ¼ cup of olive oil
- 1/3 cup of fresh lemon juice

Directions:
1. To prepare for your meal, lightly dust the chicken halves with the flour.
2. Next, heat the oil in your pressure cooker. Once this is done, sauté your chicken pieces in the hot oil until the chicken is brown on all sides. Remove the chicken from your pressure cooker.
3. Once chicken is removed, you will want to place the shallots and garlic into the oil and sauté. When they are finished, stir in the olives, basil, pepper, salt, broth, lemon juice and sherry.

4. When all of the ingredients listed above are placed in your pressure cooker, add the chicken on top and bring pressure cooker to medium-high heat to create a high pressure. Next, refuse heat to maintain the pressure.
5. Once pressure is obtained, cook the mixture for about 10 minutes.
6. Last, release pressure naturally.
7. In a separate bowl, whisk the sour cream and starch together. Spoon the sauce over your chicken for a complete meal.
8. Optional: Sprinkle cheese and add a lemon wedge for garnish.

Chicken Cacciatore

Servings:4
Total Time: 40 minutes
Ingredients:
- 3 pounds of skinless chicken breast halves
- 10 ounces of mushrooms
- 2 cups of crushed tomatoes
- 1 6 oz. can of pitted black olives
- 2 tablespoons of chopped fresh parsley
- 3 chopped shallots
- 3 chopped garlic cloves

- 1 medium green bell pepper
- 1 tablespoon of olive oil
- 2 tablespoons of tomato paste
- ½ cup of white wine
- ¼ teaspoon of crushed red pepper flakes
- ½ cup of grated parmesan cheese
- Salt and fresh ground black pepper to taste

Directions:
1. First step is to heat the olive oil in your pressure cooker. Once the oil is simmering, add the bell pepper and shallots over a medium-high heat until they begin to soften. This should take about 2 minutes.
2. Next, stir in your white wine and boil until half of it evaporates.
3. Once this is done, stir in the mushrooms and garlic then place your chicken pieces on top. When these are arranged, cover the chicken with crushed tomatoes then place tomato paste on top of that.
4. You will then want to place the lid onto your pressure cooker and bring the cooker to high pressure by using high heat. Next, reduce the heat to maintain high pressure and cook for 8 minutes.
5. Once cooked, turn the heat off and allow the pressure to come down naturally before removing the lid.
6. Last, stir in the parsley, red pepper flakes, olives, salt and pepper if desired.

Chicken Curry

Servings: 8
Total Time: 40 minutes
Ingredients:
- 8 chicken quarters
- 4 garlic cloves
- 2 large onions
- 1 green apple, diced
- 4 cups of cooked rice
- 1 cup of yogurt
- 2 tablespoons of flour
- ½ teaspoon of pepper
- 1 teaspoon of salt
- 14 ounces of chicken broth
- 2 tablespoons of olive oil
- 2 tablespoons of curry powder

Directions:
1. Begin by adding the olive oil to pressure cooker.
2. Next, brown the chicken pieces in the olive oil then remove from cooker.
3. When chicken is done, sauté onions and garlic together until they are golden brown. Once this is done, add the curry powder to the mix and begin stirring until fragrant.
4. After, add in the water, salt, pepper, and the diced green apple.

5. When all ingredients listed above are in the pressure cooker, add the chicken and place lid on pressure cooker.
6. Heat pressure cooker on high to bring to pressure and cook for about 12 minutes.
7. Next, remove the pressure cooker from heat and allow pressure to drop naturally.
8. In a bowl, combine the flour and yogurt together. Once done, pour the mixture into your pressure cooker and simmer for five minutes on low heat.
9. Once finished, combine over rice to complete your meal.

Raspberry Chicken

Servings: 4-6
Total Time: 30 minutes
Ingredients:
- 3-4 pounds of whole chicken
- 2-3 tablespoons of honey
- 2 tablespoons of soy sauce
- ½ cup of raspberry jam
- 1 teaspoon of Dijon mustard
- 1 garlic clove
- ½ cup of vinegar
- ½ cup of sweet red wine
- Optional: Orange zest garnish

Directions:
1. To start, combine honey, soy sauce, raspberry jam, Dijon mustard, garlic, vinegar, and red wine in a bowl and combine well.
2. Next, pour the mix over the chicken pieces and allow to marinate for at least four hours in a refrigerator.
3. Once marinated, place the chicken into the pressure cooker and bring to a boil.
4. After sealing, bring pressure up on high heat and cook for 20 minutes.

5. Once time has passed, remove and depressurize by using cold water.
6. If desired, serve chicken with an orange zest garnish.

Kentucky Fried Chicken

Servings: 12 pieces
Total Time: 70 minutes
Ingredients:
- 2 frying chickens, cut into 6 pieces
- 6 cups of Crisco cooking oil
- 2 cups of all-purpose flour
- 2 cups of milk
- 1 egg, beaten
- 1 teaspoon of msg
- 4 teaspoons of salt
- 2 teaspoons of black pepper

Directions:
1. In a small bowl, you will want to combine the 2 cups of milk with the egg.
2. In another bowl, combine the msg, salt, flour and black pepper.
3. Begin by dipping the chicken pieces into the milk then roll the pieces until they are completely covered by flour.
4. In your pressure cooker, pour the oil in and heat over medium- heat.
5. Place the chicken into your pressure cooker in groups of 4 or 5 and steam at pressure for about 10 minutes.

6. Next, release the pressure according to your manufacturer's instructions and repeat until all chicken is complete.

VEGETABLES

Corn on the Cob

Servings: 3
Total Time: 5 Minutes
Ingredients:
- 3 Ears of Sweet Corn cut in Half
- 1 Cup of Water

Directions:
1. In the pressure cooker, pour the cup of water into the bottom of the cooker and place the steamer insert into the cooker.
2. Next, arrange the half ears of corn into the steamer basket.
3. Secure the lid and allow cooker to come to high pressure
4. Set your timer for 2 minutes before releasing pressure. You can do so by running the cooker under cold water until the pressure releases.
5. Remove corn and enjoy your meal!

Red Potatoes
Servings: 10-12
Total Time: 13 minutes
Ingredients:

- 3 Pounds of small red potatoes. Washed and unpeeled.
- 1 Teaspoon of olive oil
- 1 Cup of water

Directions:

1. Prepare for the meal by cutting the small red potatoes into one inch cubes.
2. Next, place your cup of water and teaspoon of olive oil into your pressure cooker.
3. Set up your pressure cooker by placing a cooking rack or steamer basket into your pressure cooker.
4. Place the potatoes onto the rack or into the basket.
5. You will want to place your lid onto your pressure cooker and bring the pressure to high heat.
6. Reduce heat once pressure is achieved
7. Cook the potatoes for 3 minutes before removing the pressure cooker from the heat.
8. Use a quick release method to remove pressure from your cooker.
9. Optional: Season the potatoes with black pepper, salt, or butter.
10. Optional: Chill your cooked potatoes to produce fresh potato salad.

Butternut Squash Soup

Servings: 12
Total Time: 30 minutes
Ingredients:
- 5 pounds of butternut squash
- 1 Onion- diced
- 1 Carrot- diced
- 2 Cloves of garlic- minced
- 2 Stalks of celery- diced
- 2 Tablespoons of rosemary- chopped
- 1 Teaspoon of Paprika
- 1 Teaspoon of Nutmeg
- 4 Cups of Chicken Broth
- Optional: Salt and Pepper to Taste

Directions:
1. To prepare for your meal, sweat the onion and garlic in oil in the pressure cooker.
2. Next, add the carrots and celery to the mixture before adding the rest of the ingredients.
3. After adding the butternut squash, garlic, rosemary, paprika, nutmeg, and chicken broth, bring pressure cooker over medium heat.

4. Cook the mixture for around 20 minutes once pressure if at medium.
5. Remove the heat and release pressure by placing the cooker on the countertop.
6. It is suggested to use a hand held blender once the soup cools to smooth the consistency of the soup.
7. If you desire a thinner soup, add additional chicken broth as needed.
8. Optional: Add salt and pepper to the soup to add some spice.

White Bean Dip

Servings: 2 Cups
Total Time: 25 minutes

Ingredients:
- ¾ Cup of dried white beans or ¾ cup of navy beans
- 3 tablespoons of lemon juice
- 1/3 cup of extra virgin olive oil
- 2 cloves of garlic
- 1 ½ teaspoons of chili powder
- 1 pinch of red pepper flakes
- 2 teaspoons of ground cumin
- 3 tablespoons of cilantro
- Optional: salt and black pepper.

Directions:
1. In preparation to make your white bean dip, soak the white or navy beans overnight in water.
2. The next day, drain the beans in the pressure cooker by covering beans with at least an inch of water.
3. Next, lock the lid into place and bring the cooker to full pressure while over high heat.

4. After doing this, you will want to reduce the heat to medium to maintain even pressure.
5. Next, cook the beans for 12-13 minutes if you used white beans and 8-9 minutes if you used the navy beans.
6. After cooking the beans, remove the pressure cooker from the heat and allow the pressure to drop by itself.
7. Once the pressure is relieved, drain the beans and rinse under cold running water.
8. While the beans are cooling. Use a food processor to chop the cloves of garlic.
9. Next, add the cooled beans, olive oil, chili powder, red pepper, cumin, and lemon juice to the food processor and puree until desired smoothness.
10. If desired, add the extra salt and pepper to taste.
11. Dip goes well with fresh veggies or tortilla chips. Enjoy!

Garlic Mashed Potatoes

Servings: 6-8
Total Time: 18 Minutes

Ingredients:

- 4 Pounds of peeled potatoes
- 2 Garlic cloves or 2 tablespoons of garlic oil
- ½-3/4 Cup of warmed milk
- ¾ Cup of Water
- ¼ Cup of melted butter
- Optional: Salt and fresh ground black pepper to taste

Directions:

1. Prepare for meal by placing a trivet in the bottom of your pressure cooker.
2. Next, you will want to add the four pounds of potatoes and the water.
3. Once the product is placed, secure the lid of your pressure cooker and place over high heat to achieve high pressure.
4. Once high pressure is reached, adjust the heat to stabilize the pressure
5. Cook the potatoes for 8-10 minutes. If the potatoes are not tender at 8 minutes, bring the pressure up for the remaining time.

6. After, remove your pressure cooker from heat and allow natural pressure drop.
7. Once the pressure is relieved, remove and drain the potatoes of excess moisture.
8. In the next step, you will want to put your potatoes through a food mill or mash the potatoes by hand.
9. Next, place the mashed potatoes into a serving dish with the warmed milk until potatoes are creamy. Beat the potatoes every ¼ cup serving of milk.
10. Once smoothness level is achieved, blend in garlic and butter until completely blended.
11. If desired, season potatoes with salt and pepper to taste. Enjoy!

Tomato Soup

Servings: 4-6
Total Time: 20 minutes
Ingredients:
- 1 ¾ pounds of canned chopped tomatoes
- ½ pound of Sun-dried tomatoes
- 1 Medium peeled carrot
- 1 Medium peeled potato
- 1 Medium peeled onion
- 3 Tablespoons of tomato puree
- 4 Tablespoons of butter
- 1 Teaspoon of chopped garlic
- 1 liter of water
- Optional: 2 teaspoons of Salt
- Optional: Sour Cream if desired

Directions:
1. To begin, you will want to preheat your pressure cooker over a medium heat. DO NOT place the lid on while doing so.
2. Next, you will want to melt the butter into the pan.
3. Proceed by adding the carrots, onion, and pepper for about 5 minutes or until they soften
4. Once the carrots, onion and pepper are soft, add the canned tomatoes, tomato puree, garlic, sun-dried tomatoes, potatoes, and the water and salt.

5. When the ingredients are all in the pressure cooker, stir the mixture then place lid onto the cooker. Turn heat on high until pressure is achieved and then turn cooker down to medium heat.
6. Cook the ingredients for five minutes at full pressure.
7. Last, remove the pan from heat and allow pressure cooker to cool naturally to relieve the pressure.
8. It is suggested to use a stick blender to blend the ingredients thoroughly. If a thinner soup is desired, add more water as needed.
9. Optional sour cream garnish to compliment the soup.

Tortellini Minestrone Soup

Servings:6
Total Time: 20 minutes
Ingredients:
- 8 ounces of dry cheese tortellini
- 1 white onion, diced
- 2 carrots, sliced
- 1 can of diced tomatoes
- 2 stalks of celery, sliced
- 4 cups of vegetable broth
- 1 jar of spaghetti sauce
- 2 tablespoons of olive oil
- 1 teaspoon of sugar
- 1 ½ teaspoons of Italian seasoning
- Optional: shredded parmesan cheese

Directions:
1. In the pressure cooker, add the olive oil to the bottom and heat on high
2. Next, sauté onions, carrots, garlic, and celery until the vegetables begin to 'sweat.'
3. Once that is done, add the rest of the ingredients including: the dry cheese tortellini, can of diced tomatoes, four cups of vegetable broth, one jar of spaghetti sauce, one teaspoon of sugar, and the one and a half teaspoons of Italian seasoning.

4. Set your pressure cooker to high and cook the mixture for about five minutes.
5. Once you have cooked for five minutes, turn off the heat and use a quick release method to relieve the pressure.
6. Check the pasta to see if it is done to your liking. If not, continue cooking with the lid off until soft enough.
7. Optional: Serve minestrone soup with parmesan cheese for a garnish.

Chickpea Curry

Servings: 6
Total Time: 35 minutes
Ingredients:
- 3 cups of cooked chickpeas
- 2 cans of diced tomatoes
- 1 large sliced onion
- 4 teaspoons of crushed garlic
- 3 large potatoes, cut
- 4 teaspoons of cumin seeds
- 2 teaspoons of ground coriander
- 2 teaspoons of garam masala
- 2 teaspoons of ground turmeric
- 8 teaspoons of olive oil
- ¼ teaspoon of salt and fresh ground pepper
- ½ cup of water
- Optional: Fresh cilantro stem for garnish

Directions:
1. Begin by heating the olive oil in the pressure cooker then place cumin seeds into the oil for about 30 seconds.
2. Next, add the sliced onion and cook for 5 minutes.
3. Once the onion is golden and soft, reduce the heat and add in the garlic and other spices.

4. Once spices are stirred in together, add the remaining ingredients.
5. When everything is placed in the pressure cooker, lock the lid and bring to high pressure over high heat. Once pressure is established, cook the ingredients for 15 minutes.
6. Once cooking is complete, relieve pressure naturally and serve meal with naan or basmati rice.

Lemon Ginger Honey

Servings: 16
Total Time: 25 minutes
Ingredients:
- 1 teaspoon of fresh ginger
- 1 cup of honey
- 1 lemon

Directions:
1. Begin by placing the cup of honey into the pressure cooker mixed with hot water.
2. After, add lemon zest the fresh ginger.
3. Boil for about 10 minutes at 185 degrees
4. Remove the mixture from the heat and allow to cool for 10 minutes.
5. Stain the ingredients while it is still warm.
6. Place in jars and your lemon ginger honey is complete!

Pressure Cooked Salsa

Servings: 6 Pint Jars

Total Time: 75 Minutes

Ingredients:
- 16 cups of tomatoes
- 5 onions, chopped
- 2-3 jalapeno peppers
- 2-3 green peppers
- 24 ounces of tomato paste
- 1 cup of vinegar
- 2 teaspoons of salt
- ¼ cup of cilantro

Directions:
1. Combine tomatoes, onions, jalapenos, green peppers, tomato paste, vinegar, salt, cilantro into your pressure cooker.
2. Simmer the ingredients for about 30 minutes.
3. Allow to cool then pour into canning jars. Quick and Simple!

Clam Chowder from New England

Neck clam is the most common ingredient used in preparations in New England. Enjoy this lovely clam chowder on leisurely evening!!

Prep Time: 15 min.
Serving Size: 6

Ingredients:
- Little neck - 25 clams
- Butter - 3 tbsp.
- Diced celery - 3 stalk
- Diced bacon – 8 oz.
- Flour - 3 tbsp.
- Onion, peeled -1
- Sprig thyme - 1
- Clam broth - 6 cups
- White diced potatoes - 2
- Heavy cream - 3/4 cups

- Red pepper, diced and seeded - 1/2
- Bay leaves - 2
- Sea salt as required
- Black pepper as required

Directions:

1. At first take your electric cooker and place its inner pot. Add in bacon in the given inner pot. Press the rightful function given for making soup or stew. Cook until crisp.
2. Now mix in the butter and then vegetables. Let it cook for about 10-12 minutes. Then after mix in the flour and again cook for the next 2 minutes.
3. Now mix all other ingredients except cream. Stir them well.
4. Now close the lid on top of the Electric cooker, lock it and then close the valve given for pressure release. Press the button given to warm the food. Again press the button given for making soup or stew. Let the timer reach out to zero.
5. Then open the valve to release the entire pressure. After all the steam gets released, take off the lid.
6. At last mix in the cream. Stir it well and serve hot!!

French Soupy Onion

French soupy onion is one of the hot favorite one for pressure cooker freaks. It adds healthy value to your dining table with goodness of Swiss cheese, and toasted Italian breads. Sherry is being added to it to bring out more flavors!!

Prep Time: 12 min
Serving Size: 4

Ingredients:
- Diced onions, peeled - 4
- Sprigs thyme - 2
- Beef stock - 32 oz.
- Butter - 3 tbsp.
- Bay leaf - 1

- Black pepper - 1 tsp.
- Sea salt - 1 tsp.
- Swiss cheese - 8 slices
- Toasted Italian bread - 6 slices
- Sherry - 1/2 cup

    Directions:
1. At first take your electric cooker and place its inner pot. Press the rightful function given for making meat or chicken.
2. Now mix in the onions and butter. Stir in between till all onions cooked nicely and gets caramelized.
3. Then after mix in herbs, sherry and seasoning. Let it cook for 1-2 minute; then after pour in the stock.
4. Press the button given to warm the food. Now close the lid on top of the Electric cooker, lock it and then close the valve given for pressure release.
5. Press the rightful function given for making soup or stew. Now set the timer of the cooker at 12 minutes. Let the timer reach out to zero.
6. Then open the valve to release the entire pressure. After all the steam gets released, take off the lid.
7. On top part mix in the toasted bread, make a layer of cheese over the bread.
8. Put the lid on, close the pressure valve. Press the button given for making fish or vegetable. Let the timer reach out to zero.
9. Then open the valve to release the entire pressure. After all the steam gets released, take off the lid. Serve hot!!

Awesome Irish Stew

Irish stew prepared from lamb leg, is been used since decades in Irish preparations to add rich and aromatic flavors. Prepare this popular stew at home to enjoy all the goodness of beef stock and potatoes!!

Prep Time: 6 1/2 hours
Serving Size: 7-8

Ingredients:
- Flour - 1 cup
- Lamb leg, cubed and boneless - 64 oz.
- Baby potatoes – 16 pieces
- Onions, pearl and peeled – 20 pieces
- Beef stock - 4 cups
- Minced garlic - 8 cloves
- Red wine - 1 cup

- Sprigs rosemary - 2
- Tomato paste - 4 tbsp.
- Carrots, cut to make medium pieces - 6 large
- Bay leaves - 2
- Olive oil - 6 tbsp.
- Black pepper and sea salt as required

Directions:

1. At first take the lamb; season it nicely with pepper and salt. Now take medium sized bowl; add in flour (1 cup). Mix seasoned lamb in the bowl and mix it well with flour to coat well.
2. Then after take your electric cooker and place its inner pot. Add in oil in the given inner pot. Press the rightful function given for making chicken or meat.
3. Add the prepared lamb in heating oil; let it cook till gets browned from its sides. Take out the lamb and set aside.
4. In the inner pot; add some vegetables and allow it to cook nicely for the next 5 minutes.
5. Mix in tomato paste and again cook for about 1 minute. Now mix all the entire remaining ingredient and also add the lamb in the pot again.
6. Now close the lid on top of the Electric cooker, lock it and then close the valve for pressure release. Press the button given to warm the food. Again press the button given for making slow cooker recipes and setout timer to 6 hours. Let the timer reach out to zero.

7. Then open the valve to release the entire pressure. After all the steam gets released, take off the lid and enjoy!!

Super Duper Spaghetti Sauce

This Super Duper Spaghetti Sauce serves flavorful recipe by wrapping garlic, tomatoes, and oregano as key ingredients. The health quotient of the recipe is being added with inclusion of basil in it.

Prep Time: 50 min.
Serving Size: 2-3

Ingredients:
- Tomatoes, crushed - 2 cans
- Garlic, minced - 3 cloves
- Onion, minced - 1/2

- Oregano, chopped - 1/2 tsp.
- Basil, chopped - 1 tbsp.
- Olive oil - 2 tbsp.
- Ground pepper - 1/2 tsp.
- Water - 1/2 cup
- Sea salt - 1 tsp.
- Sugar - 1 tbsp.

Directions:
1. At first take your electric cooker and place its inner pot. Press the rightful function given for beef or chicken. Add in garlic and onions in the inner pot and sauté them.
2. Mix all remaining ingredients along with tomatoes and allow it to cook for about 5 min.
3. Carefully fill the jars with prepares sauce, keep 1 inch of space from the top.
4. Use spatula to press sauce in the jar and to release any left-over bubbles. Clean out rims with seal and white vinegar.
5. Now arrange the jars nicely in inner pot. Pour in some water till it covers 1/4 part of the jar.
6. Now close the lid on top of the Electric cooker, lock it and then close the valve for pressure release. Now press the button given for preserving or canning. Adjust time till its 45 min shows. Let the timer reach out to zero.
7. Then open the valve to release the entire pressure. After all the steam gets released, take off the lid. Use canning tongs to take out jars from inner pot.

Italian Mystery Soup

This mystery soup recipe is the gifted recipe to me by my mom, but the current version is bit of tweaked to suit modern taste culture. Prepared in a pressure cooker, it only takes around 20 minutes to get a hearty full meal; you can also freeze it and re-use it later.

Prep Time: 50 min.
Serving Size: 8

Ingredients:
- Olive oil - 2 tbs.
- Garlic, minced - 3 cloves
- Diced Onion - 1 medium
- turkey sausage (Italian) links, with removed casings - 4 pieces
- Green lentils - 1 cup

- Pearl barley - 1/2 cup
- Parsley, chopped - 1/2 cup
- Chicken breast half with removed skin - 1 piece
- Chicken stock - 3 cups
- Spinach leaves - 1 bag of around 16 oz.
- Drained chickpeas - 1 can of 15 oz.
- Mild salsa - 1 cup

Directions:

1. At first take your electric cooker and place its inner pot. Add in oil (1 tbs.) in the given inner pot. Press the rightful function given for making soup or stew.
2. Mix sausage meat, and let it cook till becomes brown colored, break them into pieces. Place the sausage in a plate and then drain out all the oil.
3. In the pot, again pour in olive oil (1 tbs.); add in garlic and onion and cook till becomes translucent.
4. Mix barley in it and stir for 1 minute. Pour in the prepared sausage. Mix in chicken, parsley, chicken stock, and lentils in the pot. Add sufficient stock till it covers up all chicken.
5. Now close the lid on top of the Electric cooker, lock it and then close the valve for pressure release. Again press the button given for making soup or stew. Set the cooker's timer to 25 minutes. Let the timer reach out to zero.
6. Then open the valve to release the entire pressure. After all the steam gets released, take off the lid.
7. Take out the chicken; shred out its meat and add them to soup. Mix salsa, spinach, and garbanzo

beans; stir the mixture to mix well. Heat again before serving.

VEGETABLES & SIDE DISH

Butternut Risotto Beauty

The popularity of Butternut Risotto is unmatched across highest rated restaurants across USA. It encircles the perfect blend of rise, basil and lots of vegetables.

Prep Time: 10 min.
Serving Size: 7-8

Ingredients:
- White onion, diced and peeled – 1 pieces
- Olive oil - 2 tbsp.
- Chicken broth - 6 cups

- Butternut squash, cubed, seeded & peeled - 2 cups
- Arborio rice - 2 cups
- Butter - 2 tbsp.
- Cheese (Romano), grated - 3 tbsp.
- Chopped Basil - 1 1/2 tbsp.
- Cinnamon- 1 medium stick
- White dry wine - 3/4 cup
- Black pepper and Salt as required

Directions:

1. At first take your electric cooker and place its inner pot. Add in butter and oil in the given inner pot. Press the rightful function given for making meat or chicken.
2. After all butter melts completely; mix in the butternut squash and onions. Cook onions for about 4 minutes, stir them in between.
3. Mix wine and rice and wine. Again cook till all wine gets absorbed. Then after, mix in cinnamon stick, chopped basil, salt, and broth.
4. Now close the lid on top of the Electric cooker, lock it and then close the valve for pressure release. Press the button given to warm the food. Now press the button given for rice or risotto. Adjust time till its 10 min shows. Let the timer reach out to zero.
5. Then open the valve to release the entire pressure. After all the steam gets released, take off the lid.
6. Finally add the cheese and then for about 30 seconds stir risotto to melt all the cheese. Serve hot!!

Quinoa Queens Pilaf

Quinoa Queens Pilaf is complete side dish that can be enjoyed with lots of ingredient combination. Feel free to experiment it by adding some of your secret ingredients.

Prep Time: 6 min.
Serving Size: 2

Ingredients:
- Quinoa - 3 cups
- Onion, diced - 1/2
- Bay leaf - 1
- Vegetable or chicken stock - 32 oz.
- Sprig thyme - 1
- Butter - 2 tbsp.

Directions:

1. At first take your electric cooker and place its inner pot. Add in butter or oil in the given inner pot. Press the rightful function given for making rice or risotto. Let it cook for the next 2 minutes.
2. In the pot, mix the Quinoa and with butter, coat it nicely. Mix all the leftover ingredients.
3. Now close the lid on top of the Electric cooker, lock it and then close the valve for pressure release. Press the button given to warm the food. Again press the button given for rice or risotto. Let the timer reach out to zero.
4. Then open the valve to release the entire pressure. After all the steam gets released, take off the lid. Enjoy hot!!

Pure Rice Pilaf

Pure Rice Pilaf is among the irresistible mouth-watering side dishes; this side kick creates heavenly fusion of vegetables, and rice. Prepare it in small potion to double its flavors and enjoyment.

Prep Time: 6 min.
Serving Size: 3-4

Ingredients:
- Vegetable or chicken stock - 32 oz.
- Rice - 3 cups
- Butter - 2 tbsp.
- Sprig thyme - 1
- Onion, diced - 1/2

- Bay leaf - 1

    Directions:
1. At first take your electric cooker and place its inner pot. Add in butter or oil in the given inner pot. Press the rightful function given for making rice or risotto. Let it cook for the next 2 minutes.
2. In the pot, mix in rice and with butter, coat them nicely. Mix in all leftover ingredients.
3. Now close the lid on top of the Electric cooker, lock it and then close the valve for pressure release. Press the button given to warm the food. Again press the button given for making rice or risotto. Let the timer reach out to zero.
4. Then open the valve to release the entire pressure. After all the steam gets released, take off the lid. Serve hot!!

Cocktail Curvy Onions

Cocktail Curvy Onions is a magical side dish to impress guests and friends over thanksgiving. Even if they are tasting it for the first time, they will become fan of it without and doubt.

Prep Time: 20 min.
Serving Size: 6-8

Ingredients:
- Pearl onions - 32 oz.
- Pepper flakes, red - 1 tbsp.
- Sugar - 3/4 cup
- White vinegar - 4 cups
- Pickling spice - 1 tbsp.

- Bay leaves - 2
- Water - 32 oz.
- Mustard seed - 1 tbsp.
- Salt - 1/4 cup

Directions:
1. At first take your electric cooker and place its inner pot. Mix in all of the mentioned ingredients (leave out chopped onions) in the given inner pot. Press the rightful function given for making meat or chicken. Let the mixture boil.
2. Now take the jars and fill them with the Pearl Onions. Carefully pour the sauce in the jars, keep 1 inch of space from the top.
3. Use spatula to press sauce in the jar and to release any left-over bubbles. Clean out rims with seal and white vinegar. Now arrange the jars nicely in inner pot. Pour in some water till it covers 1/4 part of the jar.
4. Now close the lid on top of the Electric cooker, lock it and then close the valve for pressure release. Press the button given to preserving or canning the food. Let the timer reach out to zero.
5. Then open the valve to release the entire pressure. After all the steam gets released, take off the lid. Carefully take the jars out with canning tongs.

MAIN COURSE

Cooker Magic with Chicken Sauce

Chicky chicken sauce is an easy to make in pressure cooker. It brings out subtle and tangy taste with goodness of chicken. It suits well with white rice or with stir fried broccoli.

Prep Time: 30 min.
Serving Size: 4

Ingredients:
- Whole chicken, cut to make small pieces - 48 oz.
- Dried marjoram - 1/2 tsp.
- Olive oil - 1 tbs.

- Paprika - 1/2 tsp.
- Chicken broth - 1/4 cup
- White wine - 1/4 cup
- Pepper and salt to taste

Duck sauce:
- White vinegar - 2 tbs.
- Minced ginger root - 1 1/2 tbs.
- Apricot preserves - 1/4 cup
- Honey - 2 tbs.

Directions:
1. At first take your electric cooker and place its inner pot. Add in oil in the given inner pot. Press the rightful function given for making chicken recipes.
2. In the pot, add the chicken and cook till turns brown. Take out the chicken and season it with paprika, pepper, salt, and marjoram.
3. Drain the oil; add in chicken broth and wine. Again mix the prepared chicken to the mixture.
4. Now close the lid on top of the Electric cooker, lock it and then close the valve for pressure release. Again press the button given for making chicken recipes. Let the chicken cook for about 8 minutes.
5. Then open the valve to release the entire pressure. After all the steam gets released, take off the lid. Place the chicken in serving plate.
6. In the pot, mix in honey, vinegar, apricot preserves, and ginger. Lock it again and turn on warm button. Let it cook for about 12 minutes. Till sauce becomes

thick, add the prepared sauce into chicken plate. Enjoy hot!!

Cooker Perfect Carnitas

Perfect alternative to taco bars! Carnitas easily adapts to a slow cooker technique to bring out rich aromatic flavors of pork. You can also freeze it to be enjoyed again later.

Prep Time: 90 min.
Serving Size: 12

Ingredients:
- Beef broth - 1 1/2 cups
- Canola oil - 3 tbs.
- Onion, chopped – 1 large piece
- Ground cumin - 3 tbs.
- Peppers, chopped - 2 fresh
- Ground coriander - 2 tbs.

- Pork shoulder, boneless and cut to make 1 ½ inch cubes - 3 pounds
- Garlic, chopped - 4 cloves
- Serrano pepper, chopped - 1
- Jalapeno peppers, chopped - 3

   Directions:
1. At first take your electric cooker and place its inner pot. Add in some oil in the given inner pot. Press the rightful function given for making pork recipes.
2. In the pot, add pork cubes and cook them in the oil till gets brown from its sides. Then after, mix in onion, garlic, coriander, cumin, beef broth, jalapeno, Serrano peppers, and Poblano.
3. Now close the lid on top of the Electric cooker, lock it and then close the valve for pressure release. Press the button given to warm the food. Again press the button given for making pork cuisines. Set its timer to 60-65 minutes. Let the timer reach out to zero.
4. Then open the valve to release the entire pressure. After all the steam gets released, take off the lid. Serve immediately!!